STOKES
Bird Gardening
BOOK

Stokes Field Guides

Stokes Field Guide to Birds: Eastern Region
Stokes Field Guide to Birds: Western Region
Stokes Field Guide to Bird Songs: Eastern Region
  (CD/cassette)

Stokes Beginner's Guides

Stokes Beginner's Guide to Birds: Eastern Region
Stokes Beginner's Guide to Birds: Western Region

Stokes Backyard Nature Books

Stokes Bird Feeder Book
Stokes Bird Gardening Book
Stokes Birdhouse Book
Stokes Bluebird Book
Stokes Butterfly Book
Stokes Hummingbird Book
Stokes Purple Martin Book
Stokes Wildflower Book: East of the Rockies
Stokes Wildflower Book: From the Rockies West

Stokes Nature Guides

Stokes Guide to Amphibians and Reptiles
Stokes Guide to Animal Tracking and Behavior
Stokes Guide to Bird Behavior, Volume 1
Stokes Guide to Bird Behavior, Volume 2
Stokes Guide to Bird Behavior, Volume 3
Stokes Guide to Enjoying Wildflowers
Stokes Guide to Nature in Winter
Stokes Guide to Observing Insect Lives

Other Stokes Books

The Natural History of Wild Shrubs and Vines

STOKES
Bird Gardening
BOOK

The Complete Guide to Creating a
Bird-Friendly Habitat in Your Backyard

DONALD AND LILLIAN STOKES

Range Maps by Donald and Lillian Stokes

Little, Brown and Company

Boston New York Toronto London

First Edition

Library of Congress Cataloging-in-Publication Data
Stokes, Donald W.
  Stokes bird gardening book : creating a bird-friendly habitat in your backyard / Donald and Lillian Stokes. — 1st ed.
     p.   cm. — (Stokes backyard nature book)
  Includes bibliographical references.
  ISBN 0-316-81836-4 (pbk.)
  1. Gardening to attract birds. 2. Bird attracting. I. Stokes, Lillian Q. II. Title. III. Series: Stokes, Donald W. Stokes backyard nature books.
  QL676.2.S8755   1998
  639.9'78 — dc21   97-48443

10 9 8 7 6 5 4 3 2

Design and electronic production: Barbara Werden Design

RRD-VA

Published simultaneously in Canada by
Little, Brown & Company (Canada) Limited

Printed in the United States of America

Photo acknowledgments:
Aspects, Inc.: 48
Steve Bentsen: 56, 58 right, 64 middle left, 65 bottom, 71 bottom, 92 top left
Mike Danzenbaker: 67 bottom, 70 top left, 71 top left and right, 73 top right and bottom, 78 top right, 80 top left, 85 top right, 88 bottom, 89 bottom left, 90 top left
Larry R. Ditto: 86 top right, 88 top left
Kevin T. Karlson: 30 left, 78 bottom left, 83 bottom, 84 bottom, 88 top right
Maslowski Photo: 6, 8, 22, 23 left, 25 bottom insert, 27 right, 28, 31, 39, 44, 45, 46, 49, 51, 55, 59 left and right, 63 top left and right, 63 bottom, 64 bottom, 65 middle, 68 top left and middle, 69 top left and right, 70 bottom, 72 top left, 72 bottom left and right, 73 top middle, 74 top left and right, 75 bottom left, 76 top right, 77 top left, 78 top left, 81 middle and bottom, 82 top and bottom right, 83 top left and right, 84 top right, 86 top left, 86 bottom left and right, 87 top left and bottom, 89 top left and right, 89 bottom right, 91 top left, 92 top right and bottom
Anthony Mercieca: 10, 25 top insert, 34 left, 64 middle right, 66 top left, 66 top right, 66 bottom, 67 top right, 70 top right, 75 top left, 77 bottom, 79 bottom right, 81 top, 84 top left
A. Morgan: 74 bottom left, 77 top right
Sid Rucker: 67 top left
Brian E. Small: 15 bottom, 79 top right, 82 top left
Hugh Smith III: 9, 34 right, 35, 40, 41, 65 top, 68 bottom, 72 top right, 74 bottom right, 76 top and bottom left, 78 bottom right, 79 top left, 80 top right and bottom, 82 bottom left, 85 bottom, 87 top right, 90 bottom, 91 top right and bottom
George Stewart: 23 right, 36, 47, 69 top middle, 79 bottom left
Lillian Stokes: 1, 7, 12, 13, 15 top, 16, 17, 18, 19, 20, 24, 25, 27 left, 30, 32, 37, 38, 42, 43, 50, 52, 53, 54, 55, 56, 57, 58 left, 60, 61, 69 bottom, 73 top left, 95
Tom Vezo: 11, 64 top, 68 top right, 75 top and bottom right, 76 bottom right, 85 top left, 90 top right

Contents

The Joys of Bird Gardening

What Is Bird Gardening?

At its most basic, bird gardening is planting trees, shrubs, and flowers on your property to attract birds. In a larger sense, it is trying to restore a diversity of habitats to the American landscape for the health of all living things, including ourselves.

Over the years, we have continually improved our property for birds, and it has been one of the richest experiences of our lives.

A male Rose-breasted Grosbeak on a pink flowering dogwood — a welcome visitor to any bird garden.

The Benefits to the Birds

Bird gardening helps birds survive by providing food. Birds eat all kinds of foods, and on our property we try to offer as many different types as we can. We have hedgerows that provide berries for Cedar Waxwings and Northern Cardinals. We have flowers that attract seed-eating birds like sparrows, goldfinches, and siskins. We have rich natural lawn areas that provide earthworms and other invertebrates to feed robins, bluebirds, grackles, and Red-winged Blackbirds. We have tall grass areas where voles live and this attracts Red-tailed and Red-shouldered Hawks. We have wetlands where insects breed, and that attracts swallows, swifts, flycatchers, and warblers. And we even have an area that floods in spring and attracts Solitary Sandpipers and Common Snipes during migration.

Bird gardening also helps birds breed. We have had over 35 species breed on our property, and we regularly have chickadees, titmice, nuthatches, bluebirds, swallows, sparrows, towhees, woodpeckers, warblers, thrushes, vireos, and tanagers nest and raise young in our yard. And this is just to name a few. There are also many other species that raise young in other areas nearby, and then bring them to our property afterward because of the abundance of food we have provided.

The Joys for You

The first benefit of bird gardening is getting to see the birds. We have seen over 140 species of birds on our property. People who come to our house are always amazed at how many birds are there. When we walk just a few properties away from our yard, there are very few birds; creating a good habitat really works.

Bird gardening also teaches you about the native

Asters, cosmos, and tithonia all attract birds to the seeds they produce.

plants on your own property, and not just their names but also how and where they live and what benefit they are to the birds. You will learn about the fascinating interactions between plants and birds — which plants provide food and in what season, which attract insects that the birds will then eat, which are good for nesting structures, which provide nesting materials, and which provide cover and shelter.

Bird gardening will also expand your knowledge of birds' needs — the habitats they need for breeding and feeding, the spaces they need for territories, the plants they need for nesting, and the stopover spots they need during migration.

In addition, bird gardening is active participation in conservation. By improving and diversifying the habitats in your own backyard, you are helping restore some of the natural environment that has been destroyed by human population growth and urban development. It is a positive action that each individual can do right away.

The Preservation of Nature

One of the ways to preserve valuable natural habitat is to buy it, either at the federal, state, or local level. But this can only go so far. It will always be the case that the vast majority of land is in private ownership. In the end, one of the best ways to preserve land and habitats is for each of us to do so on our own property and in our own backyard.

In addition, try to see your own yard as connected to all the other yards in your neighborhoods. By getting your neighbors interested in bird gardening you can create much larger areas of rich habitat. This will enrich the lives of your neighborhood families as well as the health of the plants and animals around you.

This sense of community — working to restore the American landscape — and rewards from providing homes and food to birds are the real joys of bird gardening.

We wish you luck with your garden and hope you attract lots of birds.

Yours,
Lillian and Don Stokes

The Four Needs of Birds

A New Way of Thinking

There are four main things that birds need from their environment: food, water, nesting spots, and shelter. If you offer these four things, you have the best chance of attracting the most birds.

To know if you have these elements on your property, you need to think from a bird's point of view. What does a bird see as food? What does a bird see as available water? Where do birds nest? And what does a bird consider shelter?

It is challenging and informative to try to think like another animal. It helps you be more sensitive to the needs of all other living things and is a great eye-opener to the principles of conservation.

A Key Concept: Diversity

As we briefly look at the four main needs of birds, we will also be constantly referring to the concept of diversity.

Nature is built upon a multitude of complex interdependencies. The more your yard can begin to reflect the variety of the natural world within a small area, the better it will support birds and other wildlife. Making a property attractive to birds through diversity will automatically make it attractive to many other types of wildlife, for they also depend upon a diversity of habitats.

#1 — Food

Birds need food. But what is food to birds? The answer is many things, including: seeds, fruits,

Creating diverse habitats that provide a wide array of foods for birds is essential to a good bird garden. This male Baltimore Oriole has found a caterpillar among the leaves of a maple tree.

There should always be water for birds to drink and bathe in. This male House Finch is enjoying a drink from a ceramic birdbath.

leaves, flowers, nectar, buds, insects, earthworms, numerous invertebrates in the earth, amphibians, reptiles, fish, mammals, and even other birds.

These foods are of two basic kinds — plants and animals. It is hard to directly affect the amount of animal food on your property, but you can easily add to the plant food and this will, in turn, attract animals.

We have suggested a variety of plant groups to create diversity, such as grasses, flowers, shrubs, and trees, all of which provide food for birds.

In our yard we try to add as many different types of plant foods as possible: flowers for nectar; grasses, flowers, and weeds for seeds; shrubs and trees for fruits; and trees for nuts. In addition, of course, we have many bird feeders.

As you look around your property, try to think like a bird. If you were a chickadee that eats insects and small seeds, where would you go? If you were a pheasant or quail that eats grains on the ground, would you have a place to feed? If you were a mockingbird that eats fruits, would you be able to find food all year? And if you were a sparrow on migration, would you stop here to eat grass and weed seeds in fall?

By thinking like this you can begin to see your property in a different light — as a large, complex living feeder for birds.

#2 – Water

Birds need water for both drinking and bathing. Is there water for birds available on your property? It is not enough that there be water; there needs to be water that birds can safely get to for drinking and shallow areas in the open where they can bathe. Having birdbaths and small pools that birds can visit is a good way to offer water. Create several, for it gives the birds choices, and it is hard to guess ahead of time which situation they will like best.

Birds also need water to drink all year, so continue to work on having water available all twelve months.

#3 – Nesting Sites

Birds need places to build a nest and raise young. As we often say, "If you don't have breeding birds, you won't have feeding birds." In other words, do not just put out feeders; provide places for your birds to breed as well.

Different species nest in different habitats and in various locations within those habitats. Therefore, you need many diverse nesting opportunities to attract a large number of nesting species.

For example, Savannah Sparrows and quail nest on the ground among tall grasses; mockingbirds, cardinals, and catbirds nest in shrubs with appropriate branching structure; robins nest on horizontal limbs of trees; orioles suspend their nests from the tips of drooping branches over open areas; titmice need birdhouses or holes in dead trees; Chipping Sparrows need dense evergreens; and Barn Swallows need access to old outbuildings or barns.

Look around your property for nests in winter (when leaves have fallen) to see what locations birds are already using for nests. And in spring and summer look for nesting birds. All properties can use more birdhouses, and most can use more diverse plantings to encourage breeding birds.

#4 — Shelter

Birds need shelter from rain, snow, sun, wind,

and predators. By providing a variety of shelter on your property you will attract more birds.

Although birds often fly around in the rain as if it were not there, during downpours they usually seek some kind of cover. We once watched a Downy Woodpecker cling to the trunk of a tree just under a larger limb throughout a heavy rainstorm. And there are many times we have seen birds during heavy rain pause under the eaves of our hopper-type feeders. Dense evergreens and large broad-leaved shrubs and trees provide birds with some protection from rain.

Dense evergreens provide good cover for birds during heavy snowfalls, and many species will fly into them and stay there until the storm is past. These evergreen shrubs or trees also keep snow from accumulating on the ground underneath them, enabling birds to look for seeds among the leaf litter. We have large rhododendrons right near our feeders and we sprinkle seed underneath them in winter. The birds use the shrubs continually, feeding on the seed and staying out of the snow.

Birds also need shelter from the sun, especially in very hot climates. We find that hummingbirds

Try to provide many different types of habitats in which birds can nest. This Yellow-rumped Warbler has chosen to nest in a dense evergreen.

Shelter is the fourth requirement of a good bird garden. Evergreens, such as this spruce, provide shelter from the wind and rain, places for birds to roost at night, and a place for this White-throated Sparrow to sing its beautiful song.

particularly like to sit in cool shade between their visits to our hummingbird feeders and nectar plants. Tall broad-leaved trees are ideal, for they provide dappled shade and let breezes go through as the birds sit on perches within them.

Strong winds can buffet birds around and cost them more energy. A windbreak or hedgerow that is planted perpendicular to the prevailing wind will attract birds, especially if feeders are placed in their lee. Birds roosting at night also need protection from chilling winds in winter. Large stands of dense evergreens provide this protection and may be used by species that roost in flocks, such as Mourning Doves and crows.

And finally, birds need protection from predators. They can usually fly away from ground predators, but they need special protection from aerial predators such as Sharp-shinned or Cooper's Hawks that attack in flight. Dense shrubs or evergreens near feeders will give the birds a way to escape the attacks of these birds of prey.

The Restoration of the American Habitat

Adding food, water, nesting spots, and shelter to the environment of your property is not something you do just to attract birds; it is much more. As we humans have gradually taken over the natural landscape for farming, roads, development, and housing we have taken away the features of the environment that birds need for their survival.

We are also dependent on these same features in the environment. But when the environment is taken away, its loss shows up more quickly in the lives of birds, for they have no alternatives. It is just a matter of time before it shows up in our own lives.

All living things on earth are ultimately dependent on the multitude of complex interdependencies of the natural world. If the birds are doing well, then we are doing well and will continue to do well. If the birds are not doing well, then in the long run, neither will we.

Enriching your own backyard is a small step that you can take to restore the American habitat, bring back the birds and other animals, and add to the long-term health of the human race in its interdependence with all other living things.

Planning and Planting Your Bird Garden

Getting Started

Undoubtedly, you want to get started right away attracting more birds to your property. You will be happy to know that no matter what the season or what size your property, there are things that you can do now to begin making your garden an Eden for birds.

For those of you who are beginners at bird gardening, this chapter will introduce you to the basics. It is divided into three sections: doing a brief inventory of your property, learning a few helpful features to garden design, and acquiring some basic gardening skills.

Doing an Inventory of Your Property

Here are some questions to ask about your own property that will help you evaluate which areas are already good for birds and which you can improve.

"What valuable plants do I own?" — Before adding or subtracting plants from your property, it is a good idea to know first what you already have. What kinds of trees, shrubs, and flowers are growing on your property? If you cannot identify them, get a friend who is better at it to walk around your yard with you and help you name them, or use some of the excellent identification guides mentioned in the Resources section at the end of this book.

Doing an inventory is not something you have to do all at once, but it can be a very rewarding part of bird gardening. It is a way to begin learning more of the wild plants around you and realizing what value they may have for birds.

In addition, it can save you money. You may already own some very valuable plants. Large trees, shrubs, and vines are especially valuable, for they can only be replaced with smaller plants, and often at considerable cost. So before cutting down what you might now consider "old bushes" and later dis-

Start by seeing what plants and habitats you already have on your property. This corner of a property already has low grass, tall grass, shrubs, and a variety of trees.

A bird-friendly garden can also follow the principles of good garden design and be beautiful to us as well as great for the birds. This garden has butterfly weed, salvia, and verbena for hummingbirds and yarrow and joe-pye weed that produce seeds for finches.

covering that they were valuable berry-producing shrubs, first find out what they are.

"What habitats do I have?" — Look at your property in terms of habitats; even a small property can have a tremendous variety. Do you have a wooded area? Do you have lawn? Do you have shrubs? Look at the soil to see where it may be rich and more moist or possibly drier and poorer. Notice where the sun rises and sets and where it shines on your property at midday. Even the position of your house can create different habitats, for there will be a shady side and a sunny side.

Also, where are there birds on your property now? What areas do they use in which seasons? And where do they seem to be most of the time?

All of these things are important to be aware of as you go about placing feeders and birdhouses and adding plants to your garden.

"What Is Next to My Property?" — Birds do not know where your property starts and ends. When deciding whether to stay in a spot, they look at a whole area and its resources. The size of the area depends on the species of bird. A House Wren may look at only a small portion of an acre before deciding to stay, but a Downy Woodpecker will be looking at 20–40 acres, and a Pileated Woodpecker will need several square miles.

Therefore, the land and habitats adjacent to your property and in your neighborhood will greatly affect the birds that come to your garden. It may also influence what you decide to do on your property. For example, if you live next to a wooded park, then you may not need to add woods, but may want to have more open space. If your neighbor has dense evergreens on your property line, then you get the advantage of their providing shelter to birds that visit your property.

You may also want to cooperate with neighbors to make certain kinds of habitats larger. A patch of blackberries could extend across two properties and be bigger and more attractive. An oak tree on one property could be matched by an oak on the adjacent property, creating a greater mass of acorns and nesting habitat. In smaller properties, where many backyards meet, this is an excellent way to overcome the limitations of space and create a much larger bird garden that all the neighbors can enjoy.

Garden Design

There is no reason why a bird garden cannot be beautiful as well as attract lots of birds. For those of you that are new to gardening and landscape design, here are a few ideas that may help make your garden and yard more pleasing.

Let Some Sun In — Plants need sun to grow and be productive. If you want plants that are healthy and produce a lot of food for the birds, then give them the sunlight they need. If your property is all wooded, then take down some trees on the southern side to let in light. If you are planting tall trees, then plant them on the north side, where they will not reduce the sunlight on your property.

Create Vistas — Try to create longer vistas from your house or from patios or seating areas that you frequent. When cutting down trees, create views; when planting trees, do not block views. These vistas can be good avenues for birds as they fly in and out of your property and they also will enable you to see more birds and follow their activities.

Create Varied Heights of Vegetation — In keeping with the idea of creating diversity on your property, try to have multiple layers of vegetation. These can be at roughly four different heights: tall trees, small trees and shrubs, flowers, and lawn or other ground covers. Arrange these layers with the tallest features in the back and the smallest layers in the front. This will be pleasing and allow you to see all of the different plants.

Get More Than One of a Plant — Many people, when starting out, buy just one of each flower or shrub. But it is often more attractive to birds if you group several of the same plant together. For example, one year we planted a Winterberry Holly in a wet area of our property. It produced lots of beautiful red berries that attracted Northern Cardinals and Cedar Waxwings that finished them off in a week. The next year, we found some more hollies on sale and bought four smaller ones to go with it. This resulted in a much larger patch. It was more visible to the birds, fed them for over a month, and created a suitable nesting habitat the next spring.

Create a Natural Effect — When planting several of the same plant, place them together in odd numbers (threes, fives, and sevens) and in a naturalistic way, rather than in a straight line. When you create a woodland edge, make it an undulating border, rather than just straight. In other words, make your yard and garden areas mirror the variety of nature. In fact, you can look to nature for design ideas.

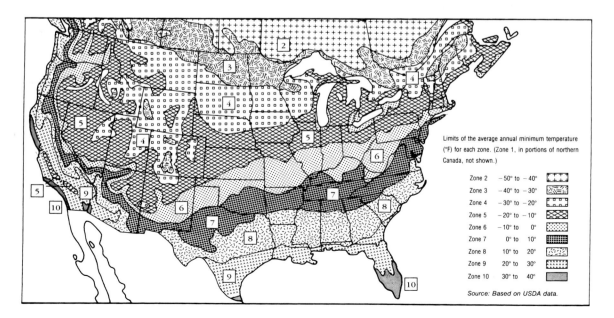

Plant Hardiness Zones

Limits of the average annual minimum temperature (°F) for each zone. (Zone 1, in portions of northern Canada, not shown.)

Zone 2	−50° to −40°
Zone 3	−40° to −30°
Zone 4	−30° to −20°
Zone 5	−20° to −10°
Zone 6	−10° to 0°
Zone 7	0° to 10°
Zone 8	10° to 20°
Zone 9	20° to 30°
Zone 10	30° to 40°

Source: Based on USDA data.

Whether you have a large or small property, try to create vistas so that you can see the birds and follow their activities in all seasons.

Make sure that your plants get lots of sunlight, good soil, and adequate water, and they will produce more food, shelter, and nesting places for birds.

Create Plantings for Year-round Beauty — Most of us do planting in spring and summer, not thinking about winter. But when planning a garden for birds, think about what your property will look like in fall and winter as well. Plant evergreen trees, shrubs, and ground covers so there will be beauty and color as well as shelter for birds in winter. Also look for shrubs and trees with colorful bark or interesting branching structure that will be pleasant to look at in winter.

Basic Gardening Skills

Some of you may already be experienced gardeners and not need this section. But for those of you that are just starting out, here are the basics of gardening.

Three Basic Needs of Plants — Plants need sun, water, and nutrients. If you give a plant these three elements, it will be healthy and productive. And, in the case of plants that provide food for birds, the more productive they are, the more birds they can feed.

Each plant has slightly different requirements for these three elements. Some plants need full sun, others can survive well in part shade. Some plants like to have their feet wet most of the time, others prefer to live in porous soil and get watered every now and then. Some plants like rich soils; others are better adapted to lesser amounts of nutrients. When buying a plant, check with your nursery to find out its requirements.

Plant Zones — Each plant also has a certain climate to which it is adapted. The most important limiting factor in this regard is the minimum temperature in the coldest season. North America has been divided into plant zones based on this minimum temperature, and all plants are rated for the zones in which they do best. Zone 1 is the coldest and zone 10 is the warmest in the United States and Canada. Zone 5 is typical of much of the Northeast, the Great Lakes states, and the mountain states. Average *minimum* winter temperatures in this zone are −10 to −20°F.

When choosing plants for your garden, check the map shown on these pages to find out what zone you live in, and then pick ones that are hardy for your zone.

In the plant lists in subsequent chapters, we mention the region of the country in which each plant tends to be grown. If you pick plants from your region and your zone, they will be the easiest to buy and the easiest to grow successfully.

How to Plant a Plant — When you buy a plant for your bird garden, you will want to be sure to give it a good start. Some of this depends on planting it in a place where it will get the sun, water, and nutrients it needs. And some of this will depend on how well you plant it.

Be sure that you have these tools on hand for gardening: a trowel, a shovel, and, if possible, a small wheelbarrow for lugging earth. Your plant, if it is fairly small, will come in a pot; if it is a shrub or small tree it may come with its roots in a ball of earth that in turn is wrapped in burlap or some other covering.

First, decide exactly where you want to put the plant by placing it in the spot and stepping back to check if it looks good. Then move the plant to the side and dig a hole a little deeper than the pot or root ball and about twice as wide.

Create a natural effect in your property by having flower beds with undulating borders and multiple layers of vegetation. This yard has grass, flower beds, shrubs, and trees all within a small area.

Create large groupings of plants and they will be more attractive to birds. This large cluster of salvias attracts hummingbirds throughout the summer with its continuous blooming.

Check the soil that you have taken out to see if it is the type of soil the plant needs. If the soil needs to be richer, mix the dug earth with some compost, which you can buy at a plant nursery. Then put some of the earth back in the hole, take the plant out of the pot or unwrap its root ball, and place it in the hole.

Make sure that the plant is the right height in the hole; the level of the earth should come to where the earth was in the pot or to the top of the root ball. Add or take away earth if adjustment is needed.

Then straighten the plant and add earth to fill in the hole. Pack down the earth firmly enough to hold the plant in place, but not too hard packed that water will have trouble getting to the roots. You can create a little well around the base of the plant to contain water and direct it to the roots.

Then water the plant well. Continue to give the plant some water the next few days and longer if the leaves show any wilting. If you want, you can add some mulch around the base of the plant in the form of bark mulch, rotted leaves, or dried grass clippings. This will help conserve moisture in the soil and keep the plant from drying out.

Caring for Plants over Time — If you do a good job gardening, your plants will grow vigorously. Amazingly, this is both a blessing and a problem. Healthy clumps of perennial flowers that were once well spaced may start to nudge one another's shoulders and compete. Successful shrubs and trees may create shade where there was once full sunlight.

In the case of the perennials, you can dig up the whole plant in fall or early spring and divide it into two or three parts with your shovel. Plant the divisions in a new area or give them to a friend to help him or her start a bird garden.

In the case of shading by trees and shrubs, either prune them back to let in sunlight, or move the plants in the newly shaded area to a spot that will be in the sun.

This is really one of our favorite features of bird gardening. Your property is always changing. You cannot hold a good and varied habitat in one stage of growth. It will mature and you have to adjust with it and learn from it.

Flowers That Attract Birds

What Flowers Offer Birds

The main attraction of flowers for birds is the seeds they produce. From late summer through winter, many flowers have dried stalks that remain standing to disperse their seeds. Most of the species that do this, such as goldenrod, aster, sunflower, and cosmos, are members of the Composite Family that produce many seeds on each flower head. This is why the birds love them — they can land at one spot and feast on all the abundance of seeds.

Some flowers typically attract a lot of insects. Examples are sedums and goldenrods. These, in turn, attract insect-eating birds like warblers and flycatchers. A few flowering plants produce berries, like baneberry, bunchberry, and jack-in-the-pulpit, but their berry production is only slight compared to that of most shrubs and trees. Wild strawberries are an exception, in that they can produce a lot of fruit early and many birds do love them; of course, so do we.

A few flowers provide nesting material. This is true of milkweeds. We grow swamp milkweed in our perennial garden and leave the stalks up until the next spring. The bark begins to peel off over winter, and in spring orioles pull off long strands to weave their suspended nests. We also have a wild stand of dogbane in our field; it is a relative of milkweeds, has the same type of bark, and orioles also visit this patch for nesting material.

Don't Cut Them Down

Many gardeners have the inclination to "tidy up" the garden in fall when blooming has stopped, by cutting·down all the stalks. But this is just when your bird garden is getting started. The standing stalks are full of seeds for the birds, and the birds will love it if you leave the stalks alone. In our garden, we leave our purple coneflower, black-eyed Susans, joe-pye weed, ironweed, cosmos, and coreopsis standing all winter and, as a result, we can always find birds in our "winter garden."

Last fall, we had up to ten goldfinches all feeding at once on our joe-pye weed. In some cases, you never quite know which plants will be attractive to the birds. For example, we had up to three Yellow-rumped Warblers on one sedum, *Sedum x* 'Autumn Joy,' seemingly getting insects or insect eggs off the underside of its flower heads. It was unexpected, but throughout fall migration, yellow-rumps were attracted to our many sedums.

Purple coneflower is not only beautiful all summer, its seed heads provide food for finches and other seed-eating birds all winter.

These sunflowers create a natural bird feeder when their seeds mature and will attract jays, grosbeaks, cardinals, chickadees, goldfinches, siskins, and many other birds.

Great Bird Garden Flowers	
	Annual/Biennial/Perennial
Bachelor's-button (*Centaurea cyanus*)	A
Cosmos (*Cosmos* spp.)	A
Love-in-a-mist (*Nigella damascena*)	A
Marigolds (*Tagetes* spp.)	A
Mexican sunflower (*Tithonia rotundifolia*)	A
Sunflowers (*Helianthus* spp.)	A
Zinnias (*Zinnia* spp.)	A
Black-eyed Susans (*Rudbeckia* spp.)	P/B
Poppies (*Papaver* spp.)	B
Asters (*Aster* spp.)	P
Blazing stars (*Liatris* spp.)	P
Coreopsis (*Coreopsis* spp.)	P
Globe thistles (*Echinops* spp.)	P
Goldenrods (*Solidago* spp.)	P
Ironweed (*Vernonia noveboracensis*)	P
Joe-pye weeds (*Eupatorium* spp.)	P
Purple coneflowers (*Echinacea* spp.)	P
Scabiouses (*Scabiosa* spp.)	P
Sedums (*Sedum* spp.)	P
Wild strawberry (*Fragaria virginiana*)	P

Annual, Biennial, Perennial

Herbaceous flowers have three basic life cycles, and it is good to be familiar with them so that you can plan where and when your flowers will grow from year to year.

Annuals live only one year and must grow from seed each year. Biennials live two years and flower in the second year, then die. Perennials continue to grow for many years but usually die back above-ground each winter and remain alive as roots.

Wild Versus Cultivated

There are both wildflowers and cultivated flowers that attract birds with their numerous seeds.

Some good wildflowers include goldenrod, yarrow, and aster. We have little patches of our property that we leave wild, and this is where we let these plants grow. But, even these areas need some management or else the shrubs will grow tall or grasses will take over. So we keep our eye on them to be sure that the bird plants we want to grow there are healthy and productive.

There are some other good wildflowers that are so lovely we put them directly in our gardens. These include ironweed, coreopsis, and purple coneflower.

We also put in our garden many cultivars of these wild plants because they bloom longer and are more prolific. These include varieties of yarrow, aster, black-eyed Susans, and joe-pye weeds.

Then there are the strictly cultivated plants we either grow from seed or buy from nurseries. Some of our favorites are cosmos, zinnia, and marigolds. These three are all annuals and need to be replaced each year.

Shrubs That Attract Birds

The Importance of Shrubs

Shrubs are extremely important to birds and one of the keys to creating a bird-friendly habitat. Shrubs are woody plants that usually grow between 3 and 15 feet tall. They are most often found at the edge of woods and in open areas such as fields, and along roads, streams, and seacoasts.

Shrubs produce fruits at different seasons. These bayberry fruits ripen in late summer, and many warblers and swallows take advantage of their high fat content to help fuel them on their fall migration.

Some shrubs also grow within open woods, where they form what is called the understory — the green area between the forest canopy and the wildflowers and other plants growing close to the ground. Forests with a good shrub understory have three different habitat layers — the tall trees, the medium-sized shrubs, and the low wildflowers and ground covers. These varied habitats support a wide variety of plants and animals. They also support many species of birds, including those species that may specialize by living in one or more of the three layers of vegetation. In eastern forests like this you will find Scarlet Tanagers and Red-eyed Vireos in the tree canopies, Wood Thrushes nesting in the shrubs, and Ovenbirds along the ground.

Wherever there are lots of shrubs, there is a good chance there are lots of birds as well. This is because shrubs provide food, nest sites, and shelter for birds — in other words, just about everything they need.

Most backyard habitats do not have enough good shrubs that birds can use. Adding shrubs that produce berries, have good nesting structure, and provide cover is a quick way to attract more birds.

Shrubs That Produce Berries and Other Food

Shrubs produce a variety of foods — berries, seeds, and nectar — and they also attract insects for the birds. You can never have too many productive shrubs on your property.

Why do plants grow berries? Berries have a fruit portion and seeds inside. The fruit portion does not help the seeds directly. The fruit attracts birds, who eat it for its sugar or fat content. The seeds, also eaten in the process, then pass through the gut of the bird and are dispersed with a little fertilizer in the dropping of the bird. Thus, berries are seed dis-

The Best Shrubs for Attracting Birds

When shrub names are plurals (for example, dog-woods), you can choose any species within that group. When names are singular (for example, American Beautyberry), that is the only species in that genus that you should use. **Region** refers to the part of the continent where the plant grows best.

Early-Summer Berries	Region
Shadbush/Serviceberry (*Amelanchier* spp.)	All
Chokecherry (*Prunus* spp.)	All
Honeysuckle (*Lonicera* spp.)	All
Manzanita (*Arctostaphylos* spp.)	NW, SW

Midsummer Berries	
Blackberries/Raspberries (*Rubus* spp.)	All
Blueberries (*Vaccinium* spp.)	All
Elderberries (*Sambucus* spp.)	All
Currants/Gooseberries (*Ribes* spp.)	All
Buffaloberries (*Shepherdia* spp.)	NW, SW

Fall Berries	
Dogwoods (*Cornus* spp.)	All
Viburnums (*Viburnum* spp.)	NE, SE, NW
Euonymus (*Euonymus* spp.)	NE, SE
Wax myrtle/Bayberry (*Myrica* spp.)	NE, SE
Mahonias (*Mahonia* spp.)	NW, SW
Madrone (*Arbutus menziesii*)	NW, SW
American beautyberry (*Callicarpa americana*)	SE
Redberry buckthorn (*Rhamnus crocea*)	SW

Winter Berries	Region
Barberries (*Berberis* spp.)	All
Sumacs (*Rhus* spp.)	All
Roses (*Rosa* spp.)	NE, SE, NW
Hollies (Ilex spp.)	NE, SE

Shrubs for Nests	
Alders (*Alnus* spp.)	All
Elderberries (*Sambucus* spp.)	All
Lilacs (*Syringa* spp.)	All
Roses (*Rosa* spp.)	All
Willows (*Salix* spp.)	All
Yews (*Taxus* spp.)	NE, NW
Spireas (*Spiraea* spp.)	NE, SE
Sages (*Salvia* spp.)	NW, SW
Saltbushes (*Atriplex* spp.)	SW
Redberry buckthorn (*Rhamnus crocea*)	SW

Shrubs for Shelter	
Junipers (*Juniperus* spp.)	All
Rhododendrons (*Rhododendron* spp.)	NE, SE, NW
Mahonias (*Mahonia* spp.)	NW, SW
Manzanitas (*Arctostaphylos* spp.)	NW, SW
Redberry buckthorn (*Rhamnus crocea*)	SW
Leucothoes (*Leucothoe* spp.)	NE, SE, NW

Shrubs with Seeds	
Alders (*Alnus* spp.)	All

persal mechanisms for the shrub, thanks to the birds.

Most berries are produced on shrubs, although a few trees and wildflowers also produce them. Berries are small fruits and they may have evolved just for birds. They are colorful, relatively odorless, and grow at the tips of thin branches. This is perfect for birds, for they see color, have little sense of smell for the most part, and are light and can get to the tips of branches. Larger fruits, such as apples, probably evolved primarily for mammals. They are large, fall to the ground, and usually ferment and give off a strong odor, thus attracting mammals that have a well-developed sense of smell.

Different species of shrubs produce berries at varying times of year. When planning your backyard habitat, you want berries available to birds in each season. There are plants like honeysuckle, shadbush, and chokecherry that produce berries early in summer. Then there are good mid- to late-summer berry-producing shrubs, such as blackberry, blueberry, huckleberry, and elderberry. Shrubs that produce berries in fall include bayberry, viburnum, juniper, holly, and manzanita. These fall

This male Eastern Bluebird is perched on staghorn sumac fruits. Sumac fruits ripen in fall, and bluebirds depend on them as food throughout the winter.

berries can be extremely important to migrating birds. This is particularly true of bayberry, which produces a waxy fruit. The high fat content of this berry enables many species that migrate along the coasts, such as warblers and swallows, to accumulate the fat reserves needed for their long journeys.

And if you observe carefully, you will see that some shrubs produce berries in fall but they are not eaten until winter; this would include sumac and rose. By also having these types of shrubs in your yard, you can offer birds berries all year.

When planting berry-producing shrubs, try to plant 3–5 of each variety. This way you can have a substantial quantity of berries for the birds and outlast the first flock that visits.

Shrubs can produce many more berries if they get enough sunlight and are not overcrowded. Maintain the health of your shrubs by pruning back competing plants around them. Trees can shade shrubs that need lots of sunlight. By cutting them back and giving the shrub sunlight, you may be able to double its berry production, resulting in a tremendous help to the birds.

In other cases, when a shrub is too crowded or not growing vigorously, it may need to be moved to a new situation. If so, review its growing requirements and transplant it to a more suitable part of your property. This will make the plants on your property more productive.

In addition to producing berries, shrubs attract a lot of insects on which birds can feed. These include bees and flies attracted to the pollen and nectar in the flowers, and caterpillars, beetles, and bugs attracted to eating the leaves. These insects are a major source of food to birds and should be left alone and not exterminated. Birds especially need insects when breeding, for they feed them to their young as a source of protein.

There are also many shrubs that attract hummingbirds, which come to drink the nectar from their flowers. For more on these plants, see the chapter Creating a Hummingbird Garden.

A few shrubs produce seeds that are eaten by birds. We have many alders growing in the wet areas of our property, and the goldfinches and Tree Sparrows feed on these seeds all winter.

Shrubs as Nesting Sites

Many of our backyard birds prefer to nest in shrubs. Shrubs offer sites that are off the ground but still protected from the winds and exposure associated with tree canopies.

However, just by planting shrubs you do not automatically provide nesting places for birds. This is because the branching structure of the shrub has to be the right density to support the nest. If branching is too open or sparse, then there is no place to build the nest. This is true for many rhododendrons and some viburnums where there is never a three-way fork in the branches on which the bird can build the nest.

In some other cases, the shrub may be so densely branched, or full of thorns, that the bird cannot get into the interior portion. We have had several barberry shrubs that were too dense, leaving no room for a nest, and we have had hawthorns that had many thorns too long for the birds to maneuver around.

Shrubs we have found good for bird nests on our property include elderberry, rose, dogwood, alder, and willow. An additional nesting use for willows is that some birds, such as Yellow Warblers, collect the fluffy seed dispersal filaments in spring and use them as the main material for their nest.

The placement of shrubs is also important in

Blackberries mature their fruits in early summer and are a great source of food for many birds, including this male Northern Cardinal.

Viburnums are very productive native shrubs. This highbush cranberry is a type of viburnum that matures fruits in late summer, and the Cedar Waxwing here is a juvenile, which you can tell because of its streaked breast.

attracting nesting birds. Lone shrubs in the middle of an open area are not as attractive as groups of shrubs or shrubs placed in association with trees or in among taller wildflowers. These groupings of plants offer more protection from the elements and predators and a greater area in which to gather food items.

Shrubs are also the mainstay of a hedgerow. For more on this see the chapter 8 Easy Things to Do That Will Attract Birds.

Shrubs as Shelter

Shrubs are also important to birds as shelter. They can create wonderful protection from wind, rain, cold, snow, and predators. Obviously, evergreen shrubs provide year-round shelter. We plant rhododendrons near our bird feeders and the birds love them. They fly into them as a first stop before coming to the feeders. They dart for cover among them when they perceive danger in the area. And many ground-feeding species, such as towhees, thrushes, and native sparrows, like to scratch around beneath them in the fallen leaves to look for seeds or insects.

Other evergreen shrubs that are good for shelter include juniper and holly (which also produce berries), laurel, and leucothoe. Deciduous shrubs are equally important as summer shelter for all of our nesting birds, providing protection from sun, relief from heat, and safe places for fledglings to perch while waiting for their parents to arrive with food.

Vines That Attract Birds

How Vines Work

Woody vines are an interesting type of plant, for they depend on other larger structures, like trees and shrubs, for their physical support. A vine cannot support itself in such a way that it can get taller and compete for sunlight. Therefore, it grows up shrubs and trees and any other supports it can find in order to satisfy its sunlight needs.

Thus, every vine needs a way to hold on to other structures. Some vines, like honeysuckle and bitter-sweet, twine around their supports. Other vines, like catbrier and grape, have tendrils that wrap around smaller branches and supports. And a few vines, such as poison ivy and Virginia creeper, grow tendrils or rootlike structures that actually attach to their supports with little roots or adhesive disks.

Vines provide food, shelter, nesting sites, and even nesting material for birds.

Vines That Provide Food

Many of our vines produce berries that birds love. These include Virginia creeper, honeysuckle, catbrier, grape, and poison ivy. On our property we encourage catbrier, Virginia creeper, and grape, and we tolerate poison ivy in restricted areas where it will not harm anyone.

Interestingly, of these vines, the most popular among birds is poison ivy, which produces large quantities of small white berries in fall. It seems strange that a plant so toxic to our skin when we touch it does not bother the birds at all. At least 55 species of North American birds are known to eat poison ivy fruits. The birds, of course, disperse the seeds in their droppings, and this is why poison ivy seems to grow everywhere.

There are a few vines that are also favorites of hummingbirds because they offer nectar for the birds to eat. These include trumpet honeysuckle and trumpet vine. As their names suggest, both have long tubular red flowers that are especially attractive to hummingbirds.

Nest Sites and Shelter

On our property we have a wonderful area filled with catbrier. The catbrier grows up the trees and has created a dense thicket that is impenetrable by us. To many, it might look like an overgrown and

The Best Vines for Birds	
Best Vines with Berries	**Region**
Honeysuckles (*Lonicera* spp.)	All
Bittersweet (*Celastrus scandens*)	NE, SE
Grapes (*Vitis* spp.)	All
Poison ivy (*Rhus radicans*)	All
Greenbriers (*Smilax* spp.)	NE, SE, NW
Virginia creeper (*Parthenocissus* spp.)	All
Carolina snailseed (*Cocculus carolinus*)	NE, SE
Supplejack (*Berchemia scandens*)	SE
Best Vines for Shelter, Nests, and Nesting	
Greenbriers (*Smilax* spp.)	NE, SE
Grapes (*Vitis* spp.)	All
Best Vines for Hummingbirds	
Trumpet honeysuckles (*Lonicera* spp.)	All
Trumpet vine (*Campsis radicans*)	NE, SE
Cross vine (*Bignonia capreolata*)	SE
Coral vine (*Antigonon leptopus*)	SE

Here is a female Northern Cardinal enjoying wild grapes. Cardinals not only eat the fruits, they also use strips of grape bark in the lining of their nest.

Virginia creeper is a good native vine that produces lots of blue berries in fall, when its leaves also turn brilliant red.

untended area, but we know it is a haven for birds. There are always birds in and among the stems, sunning, resting, feeding on the berries or on the ground beneath. And when winter comes and all the leaves fall off the vines, we always see one or more nests that were built and used during the previous summer and remained hidden until this time. It is a good safe place for the birds.

Another interesting use of a vine is as nest material. Grape vines have bark that peels off easily and is very flexible. The bark is also easy to split into finer strands. Many birds take advantage of this material and its properties and use the bark as part of their nest. Catbirds, mockingbirds, and cardinals use it in the main structure of their nest, and smaller birds, such as goldfinches, vireos, and sparrows, take finer strands and use them as part of their nest lining. It is worth having grape vines just for their attractiveness as a nesting material.

Managing Vines

Vines, by their very nature, are slightly unman-

ageable, for they are climbing up other plants and, in some cases, shading them out. The best place to have vines is on some part of your property where you do not mind if they take over, such as up a dying tree or as part of a hedgerow.

Another great way to use vines is along a fence, such as a chain-link or wooden fence. The vines will use the support, hide the fence, and be a resource for the birds. Vines on a fence can also create a screen from another area, such as a compost pile, and hide that area in the summer months when you are most often outside. If the fence is like a stockade fence and too smooth for the vine to attach itself, you can hammer a few nails into the fence or place some fine netting on the fence; the vine will use this as a way to climb up the support.

We grow honeysuckle vines along a split-rail fence and also grow some on teepees of stakes in the garden for hummingbirds. In the garden, they need to be pruned back to stay in control. We also have grape vines in our hedgerow and American bittersweet growing along a wire-mesh fence.

Trees That Attract Birds

Trees That Supply Food for Birds

Trees supply a vast variety of foods for birds, not only because of the seeds and fruits that they produce, but also because of the insects they attract.

Small Seeds — Many trees produce seeds that birds eat. Some of these seeds are extremely small, such as those of birches, which are produced in catkins at the tips of the branches. These are eaten by many small birds, including goldfinches, Pine Siskins, and redpolls, that can hold on to the tips of the fine branches and not weigh them down too much.

Large Seeds — Most trees produce larger seeds.

These include elms, tulip poplars, ashes, and many of the coniferous evergreens such as hemlock, pine, spruce, and fir. Ash and tulip poplar seeds are eaten by birds with large conical beaks especially designed for shelling off the husk of these seeds. Cardinals, grosbeaks, and Evening Grosbeaks all can be found in the tops of these trees, seemingly glued to the branches as they pick off, shell, and eat the tree seeds one after another.

The seeds in conifers are harder to access because they are inside a cone with tough scales that protect the seeds. Seeds in smaller cones, like those of hemlocks, can be taken directly out of the cone by birds like chickadees, nuthatches, and titmice, but in order for birds to get the seeds in larger cones, they usually have to first pry apart the

This male Eastern Bluebird depends on berries to get through the winter, and this holly tree is a good source of winter fruits.

The Best Trees to Attract Birds

Try to have trees from all 5 categories in your yard and maximize diversity whenever possible. When tree names are plurals (for example, Pines) you can choose any species within that group. When names are singular (Red Mulberry, for example), that is the only species in that genus that you should use. Region refers to the general area in which the plant grows best. Check your local nursery for more detailed growing conditions in your specific location.

Best Fruit Trees	Region
Cherries (*Prunus* spp.)	All
Hackberries (*Celtis* spp.)	All
Junipers/Red cedar (*Juniperus* spp.)	All
Red mulberry (*Morus rubra*)	All
Crabapples (*Malus* spp.)	NE, SE, NW
Hawthorns (*Crataegus* spp.)	NE, SE, NW
Mountain ashes (*Sorbus* spp.)	NE, SE, NW
Dogwoods (*Cornus* spp.)	NE, SE
Hollies/Possumhaw (*Ilex* spp.)	NE, SE
Madrone (*Arbutus* spp.)`	NW, SW
Cabbage palm (*Sabal palmetto*)	SE
Strangler fig (*Ficus aurea*)	SE

Best Seed Trees	
Maples/Box elder (*Acer* spp.)	All
Pines (*Pinus* spp.)	All
Spruces (*Picea* spp..)	All
Birches (*Betula* spp.)	NE, SE, NW

	Region
Firs (*Abies* spp.)	NE, NW, SW
Hemlocks (*Tsuga* spp.)	NE, NW
Larches (*Larix* spp.)	NE, NW
Ashes (*Fraxinus* spp.)	NE, SE
Tulip tree (*Liriodendron tulipifera*)	NE, SE

Best Shelter Trees	
Junipers (*Juniperus* spp.)	All
Pines (*Pinus* spp.)	All
Spruces (*Picea* spp.)	All
Firs (*Abies* spp.)	NE, NW, SW
Hemlocks (*Tsuga* spp.)	NE, NW
Mesquites (*Prosopis* spp.)	SW

Best Cavity Trees	
Aspens (*Populus* spp.)	All
Cottonwoods (*Populus* spp.)	All
Oaks (*Quercus* spp.)	All
Sycamores (*Platanus* spp.)	All
Apples (*Malus* spp.)	NE, SE, NW
Birches (*Betula* spp.)	NE, SE, NW
Ashes (*Fraxinus* spp.)	NE, SE
Willows (*Salix* spp.)	NE, SE
Poplars (*Populus* spp.)	NE, NW

Best Nut Trees	
Oaks (*Quercus* spp.)	All

scales. Some birds, such as crossbills, have bills that are crossed at the tip and especially designed for prying apart the scales of cones; they then reach in with their tongues to get the seeds.

Berries — Many trees produce berries or larger fruits. Berry-producing trees include mountain ash, dogwood, cherry, mulberry, and manzanita, to name a few. These trees often produce larger quantities of berries than shrubs and can be a good source of food over a long period of time. Most trees produce berries that ripen in fall and are available to birds in fall and winter. A few, such as cherry and mulberry, develop berries earlier, and these are useful in attracting large flocks of birds in mid- to late summer.

Nuts — Some trees produce large nuts that birds eat. The most important and widespread of these are the oaks. Acorns are heavily used by Wood Duck, grouse, quail, Band-tailed Pigeon, Wild Turkey, jays, grackles, thrashers, and some woodpeckers. One problem with oaks for animals is that these trees have some seasons of heavy production and others of sparse production. Many birds, such as Mexican Jays and Acorn Woodpeckers, take the acorns and store them in the ground or the crevices of trees. Acorn Woodpeckers make their living this way, actually excavating holes in trees or buildings and jamming the acorns into them.

Insects — Trees are also essential for birds because of the insects they attract. Many birds, such as warblers, vireos, and orioles, glean insects off the tree leaves and flowers. All trees have flowers, but many are inconspicuous and appear in the form of tassels called catkins. Catkins of some trees attract lots of flies and other small insects. This is particularly true of oaks, whose flowers bloom in spring, when warblers migrate through most of the lower 48 states. On our property we have made a point of saving lots of oaks and, as a result, we get to see many warbler species in spring.

Oak leaves also attract numerous species of flies and wasps that form galls — small deformations of the plant growth that insects live inside. These galls occur all summer and fall, and chickadees, woodpeckers, and other small birds peck them open to get at the insects. More galls form on oaks than on any other group of plants.

Many insects use bark crevices as a protected place to lay their eggs, develop, or overwinter. Birds like nuthatches, chickadees, warblers, woodpeckers, creepers, and wrens repeatedly search every inch of tree bark for these insects. Oak, hickory, cherry, cottonwood, and ash are trees with furrowed bark that attract insects and thus the birds. Trees with smooth or continuously peeling bark, like birch, beech, and cedar, may be less productive in this way.

Many trees also create a lot of debris under them, such as leaves, flower parts, and seeds. This leaf litter provides a good place for beetles, ants, and other insects to live. Sparrows, towhees, grackles, thrushes, and quail like to scratch around in this litter for seeds and insects.

Trees for Nesting Birds

Trees help birds nest in a variety of ways. Their branches are used for nest support. Crows and hawks nest in the crotches of large branches where they split off from the trunk. Robins, tanagers, grosbeaks, and other birds their size prefer to nest farther out, often where several smaller branches grow off a larger branch and provide a good plat-

Evergreen trees, such as pine, produce cones with seeds that birds like this Black-capped Chickadee eat. Evergreen trees also provide shelter and seem to attract overwintering insects, which chickadees, nuthatches, kinglets, and creepers continually glean.

Mountain ashes produce a lot of berries in northern latitudes, helping birds survive the cold.

Flowering dogwoods are not only one of our most beautiful native trees, they also produce red fruits that birds, such as Blue Jays, eat in late summer.

form. Vireos and orioles like to nest even farther out, where they suspend their nest beneath the finer branch tips.

Trees are also the main home for cavity-nesting birds. Woodpeckers are the primary excavators of these holes. Downy Woodpeckers prefer to excavate in dead wood, while Hairy Woodpeckers usually excavate in live wood. It is important to keep a mix of both dead and live limbs on standing trees, as long as it is safe for humans.

After woodpeckers make the holes, other birds like bluebirds, wrens, Tree Swallows, and nuthatches use the abandoned holes for their own nests. Thus, any tree hole on your property is important to keep, for many birds may use it in successive years.

Some trees have a tendency to rot where branches have broken off, or decay in their heartwood. This provides softer wood where cavity-nesting birds like chickadees may be able to excavate their own nest hole. Trees with this characteristic include birch, apple, ash, oak, poplar, aspen, and willow.

Birch and cedar, as well as a few other species,

have fine, peeling bark, and many birds gather this off the tree trunk to use in their nests.

Trees for Shelter

Trees are also an important way of providing shelter for the birds on your property. Of course, evergreens provide year-round shelter for birds from cold, rain, and snow; hidden places for nests; hiding places from predators; and even daytime roosts, such as where an owl might hide for the day out of sight from harassing crows and jays.

You can also plant evergreens along the north side of your property. In winter, they will protect feeders from the north winds and also absorb the low southern sun, creating a warmer mini-habitat for the birds on the south side.

Trees can also be planted as a windbreak or snowbreak between two fields and become a place where the birds can take advantage of the food in the fields while still having the protection of the trees.

Creating a Hummingbird Garden

Hummingbirds and Flowers

Hummingbirds have a closer relationship to flowers than any of our other birds. Both their form and flight are intricately coevolved with the species of flowers from which they drink nectar.

Flowers produce nectar to attract pollinators, which inadvertently carry their pollen from one flower to the next. This fertilizes the flowers, which then develop seeds.

Cardinal flower is a native plant that hummingbirds love. In the wild, it grows along slow-moving streams, but it can also be grown in a moist, partially shaded portion of your bird garden. Goldfinches eat the seeds in fall.

You can recognize a flower specifically adapted to hummingbirds by three things. First, they are red, a color easily seen by birds but appearing just dark, and not as attractive, to bees and other insects. Second, they have evolved long tubes that only hummingbirds with their long bills and tongues can get into. And last, they orient their flowers horizontally, for hummingbirds can hover perfectly while they drink the nectar, but bees and butterflies cannot hover as well.

Hummingbirds are particularly attracted to flowers with these adaptations because they are most assured that there will be a meal for them. But they will also visit all other flowers in their search for nectar.

Hummingbird flowers have also evolved their stamens to get pollen on the hummingbird at just the right place. Most hummingbird flowers get pollen on the forehead of the bird; these include cardinal flower, penstemons, and paintbrushes. Arizona trumpet gets pollen on the hummingbird's chin. And flowers like columbine and currant get pollen all around the base of the bird's bill.

Elements of a Good Hummingbird Garden

A good hummingbird garden has more than just hummingbird flowers. It is a whole habitat in which the hummingbirds will want to stay. Here are some of the elements of that habitat.

Be sure to have a mixture of sun and shade in your garden, created by a few trees and open areas. The flowers will need the sun to grow and the hummingbirds will need shade to perch in between feedings.

Have different levels of vegetation, including tall trees, medium-height trees, shrubs, and flowers. Hummingbirds also like to perch in spots where

Nursery Plants for Hummingbirds

Herbaceous plants

Bee balms (*Monarda* spp.)
Begonias (*Begonia* spp.)
Blazing stars (*Liatris* spp.)
Bleeding hearts (*Dicentra* spp.)
Butterfly-weed (*Asclepias tuberosa*)
Canna (*Canna generalis*)
Cardinal flower (*Lobelia cardinalis*)
Carpet bugle (*Ajuga reptans*)
Century plant (*Agave americana*)
Columbines (*Aquilegia* spp.)
Coral-bells (*Heuchera sanguinea*)
Dahlia (*Dahlia merckii*)
Dame's rocket (*Hesperis matronalis*)
Delphiniums (*Delphinium* spp.)
Fire pink (*Silene virginica*)
Flowering tobacco (*Nicotiana alata*)
Four-o'-clock (*Mirabilis jalapa*)
Foxgloves (*Digitalis* spp.)
Fuchsias (*Fuchsia* spp.)
Gilias (*Gilia* ssp.)
Geraniums (*Pelargonium* spp.)
Gladiolus (*Gladiolus* spp.)
Hollyhocks (*Althaea* spp.)
Impatiens (*Impatiens* spp.)

Lantana (*Lantana camara*)
Lilies (*Lilium* spp.)
Lupines (*Lupinus* spp.)
Nasturtium (*Tropaeolum majus*)
Paintbrushes (*Castilleja* spp.)
Penstemons (*Penstemon* spp.)
Petunias (*Petunia* spp.)
Phlox (*Phlox* spp.)
Red-hot poker (*Kniphofia uvaria*)
Scabiouses (*Scabiosa* spp.)
Scarlet sage (*Salvia splendens*)
Spider flower (*Cleome spinosa*)
Sweet william (*Dianthus barbatus*)
Verbenas (*Verbena* spp.)
Yuccas (*Yucca* spp.)
Zinnias (*Zinnia* spp.)

Shrubs

Abelia (*Abelia grandiflora*)
Azaleas (*Rhododendron* spp.)
Bearberry (*Arctostaphylos* spp.)
Beauty bush (*Kolkwitzia amabilis*)
Beloperone (*Beloperone californica*)
Butterfly bush (*Buddleia davidii*)

Cape honeysuckle (*Tecomaria capensis*)
Currant (*Ribes odoratum*)
Flowering quince (*Chaenomeles japonica*)
Gooseberry (*Ribes speciosum*)
Hardy fuschia (*Fuschia magellanica*)
Hibiscus (*Hibiscus* spp.)
Honeysuckles (*Lonicera* spp.)
Jasmines (*Jasminum* spp.)
Scarlet bush (*Hamelia erecta*)
Weigelas (*Weigela* spp.)

Vines

Cypress vine (*Quamoclit* spp.)
Honeysuckle (*Lonicera heckrottii*)
Morning glories (*Ipomoea* spp.)
Scarlet runner bean (*Phaseolus coccineus*)
Trumpet vine (*Campsis radicans*)
Trumpet honeysuckle (*Lonicera sempervirens*)

---

they have a view of all the flowers and the general area. These varied heights of vegetation give them a good choice of perches. The different levels also create varied habitats that will attract insects on which hummingbirds also feed.

Plant lots of hummingbird flowers. Try to have species that bloom at different times so that nectar is offered over several months; and create large groups of each species so that they will offer more nectar and be visually attractive to the hummingbirds.

Like all birds, hummingbirds need water for drinking and bathing and this can be offered in a birdbath. If a mister is placed in the middle of the bath, sometimes hummingbirds will fly through it to bathe. They also can bathe in the spray from a sprinkler system. In the morning they may drink water from dewdrops on leaves.

Hummingbirds nest in a variety of habitats. To build their nest, most species need downy fibers, which form the bulk of the nest; spider silk, which is used to hold the fibers together; and lichens, which they attach to the outside of the nest to make it camouflaged. Planting willow shrubs, whose downy seed dispersal filaments are used for nesting by hummingbirds, may help attract the birds.

The Flowers

There are many ways to create a hummingbird garden with flowers. One of the simplest is to buy several containers, like pots and barrels, group them together on a patio, path, or deck, and plant hummingbird flowers in them. We do this on a patio outside our kitchen. Sometimes we place a hummingbird feeder right near the flowers as well.

Another easy way to create a hummingbird garden is to add some hummingbird flowers to an existing garden. Hummingbirds are aggressive and they will try to defend a single patch of flowers, but if you space your flowers out around your yard, you may be able to accommodate more hummingbirds.

We have listed plants that are native wildflowers in the West or in the East. These are available from native wildflower societies and sometimes from nurseries. In addition, we have listed common nursery plants that are also attractive to hummingbirds.

Hummingbird Feeders

In addition to flowers, you can have hummingbird feeders. These can be very attractive to the birds and are often a more consistent source of food than flowers.

Hummingbird feeders come in two basic models: feeders that work on a vacuum principle and are essentially bottles turned upside down into a dish; and feeders that are a simple dish. The latter are easy to fill and convenient to clean.

Hummingbird feeders should be filled with a clear sugar water solution that is easy to make in your own kitchen. Simply add four parts water to one part sugar; for example, a cup of sugar to four cups of water. Boil for several minutes and then cool. Pour the cooled liquid into the feeder and store any extra in the refrigerator. Use only pure white table sugar, never brown sugar, raw sugar, or honey, as these may ferment more easily and could harm the birds. No red dye is necessary to attract the birds, since there is red on the feeders, and it is not fully known what effect the dye may have on the birds.

Change the solution and clean out the feeder with hot water every 2–3 days so that no mold ever grows inside.

This male Ruby-throated Hummingbird is taking nectar from Indian paintbrush, a native wildflower with many different species, most of which are loved by hummingbirds.

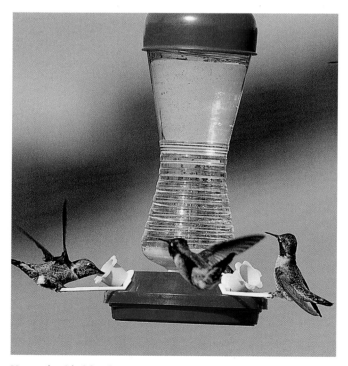

Hummingbird feeders are a great way to supplement the hummingbird flowers in your garden. Here are several female Anna's Hummingbirds competing for sugar water at a feeder.

Wildflowers for Hummingbirds

Western Wildflowers

Arizona trumpet (*Zauschneria latifolia*)

Bee balms (*Monarda* spp.)

Bleeding hearts (*Dicentra* spp.)

Calico bush (*Lantana horrida*)

California figwort (*Scrophularia californica*)

California Indian pink (*Silene californica*)

Cardinal flower (*Lobelia cardinalis*)

Columbines (*Aquilegia* spp.)

Coral bean (*Erythrina herbacea*)

Coral gilia (*Gilia subnuda*)

Desert lantana (*Lantana macropoda*)

Desert trumpet (*Ipomopsis aggregata*)

Devil's bouquet (*Nyctaginia capitata*)

Grand collomia (*Collomia grandiflora*)

Lady Bird's centaury (*Centaurium texense*)

Lilies (*Lilium* spp.)

Mexican pink (*Silene laciniata*)

Monkey flowers (*Mimulus* spp.)

Mountain centaury (*Centaurium beyrichii*)

Red figwort (*Scrophularia coccinea*)

Red fireweeds (*Epilobium* spp.)

Red paintbrushes (*Castilleja* spp.)

Red penstemons (*Penstemon* spp.)

Red Phlox (*Phlox* spp.)

Rock gilia (*Gilia scopulorum*)

Scarlet betony (*Stachys coccinea*)

Scarlet creeper (*Ipomoea hederifolia*)

Scarlet delphinium (*Delphinium cardinale*)

Scarlet sages (*Salvia* spp.)

Snow plant (*Sarcodes sanguinea*)

Texas mallow (*Malvaviscus arboreus*)

Tiny trumpet (*Collomia linearis*)

Eastern Wildflowers

Bee balm (*Monarda didyma*)

Canada lily (*Lilium canadense*)

Cardinal flower (*Lobelia cardinalis*)

Cross vine (*Bignonia capreolata*)

Fire pink (*Silene virginica*)

Fireweed (*Epilobium angustifolium*)

Indian paintbrush (*Castilleja coccinea*)

Indian pink (*Spigelia marilandica*)

Pale jewelweed (*Impatiens pallida*)

Purple bergamot (*Monarda media*)

Red iris (*Iris fulva*)

Red morning glory (*Ipomoea coccinea*)

Red turtlehead (*Chelone obliqua*)

Scarlet lychnis (*Lychnis chalcedonica*)

Smooth phlox (*Phlox laberrima*)

Spotted jewelweed (*Impatiens capensis*)

Texas plume (*Ipomopsis rubra*)

Trumpet honeysuckle (*Lonicera sempervirens*)

Trumpet vine (*Campsis radicans*)

Wild columbine (*Aquilegia canadensis*)

Wild sweet william (*Phlox maculata*)

Wood lily (*Lilium philadelphicum*)

You can place your hummingbird feeder anywhere outside. It can hang off the eaves or from a deck; it can be in a garden or by itself. We often hang our feeders off poles that we stick in the ground near our hummingbird flowers and usually in a location where we can see them from inside the house.

Fuchsias are readily available at garden centers and are easy to grow in the ground or hanging pots. This Anna's Hummingbird is attracted to the blossoms for nectar.

8 Easy Things to Do That Will Attract Birds

If you are like us, you will want to do everything possible to get more birds to visit your property. In addition to bird gardening, there are several other little tricks. What follows are some of these tricks. Do any or all of them and you will increase your chances of attracting birds.

Create a Brush Pile

There are many reasons birds love brush piles:

If you leave dead trees and dead limbs standing, they attract insects, which in turn attract birds that eat them, such as this male Downy Woodpecker.

they provide cover, there are insects among the decaying branches or on the ground beneath, and there are often seeds caught within the spaces after being blown by the wind. Some birds, like Carolina Wrens, may even nest in a brush pile.

A good way to make a brush pile is to take fallen limbs and pruned branches from trees and shrubs on your property and loosely stack them in an area where they will not be obtrusive to you or your neighbors. The pile should be about 10 feet by 6 feet to attract the birds. It should always be airy and have lots of open spaces for small birds to flit in and out. It should not be mixed with soft vegetation, for this will fill the spaces and rot.

Our brush piles are used most often in winter and visited by Song Sparrows, White-throated Sparrows, American Tree Sparrows, Dark-eyed Juncos, House Wrens, Winter Wrens, Carolina Wrens, Black-capped Chickadees, and Tufted Titmice.

Put Up a Bird Planting Wire

A good way to add to your bird garden is to let the birds choose and plant the plants. You can do this by stringing a clothesline or sturdy wire out in the open between 2 points, either 2 trees or 2 posts. Make it at least 10–20 feet long and over 6 feet high so no one will walk into it.

What happens is that birds will start to land on the wire and while they perch there, their droppings will fall below. Any seeds excreted in their droppings will be planted in the ground beneath. Over time, you will get a selection of berry-producing plants that the birds obviously like. This is not a quick way to a bird garden, but it is a nice way to let the birds have a say in what gets planted in your yard. The only caution is that some of the plants that arrive via the birds may be invasive

Planting a hedgerow that contains a variety of shrubs is a wonderful way to provide food, shelter, and nesting habitats for many species of birds.

exotics and they should be weeded out. See the chapter Invasive Exotics and Natural Natives.

Birds that will help plant your garden include Northern Mockingbird, American Robin, Gray Catbird, bluebirds, and Cedar Waxwing.

Let Dead Trees Stand

Dead trees and limbs are a wonderful source of food and homes for birds. As trees or limbs start to die, many insects use the loosened bark as sources of food, places to lay eggs, and places to overwinter. In addition, some insects, such as beetles, will start to bore into the bark and the wood of the tree.

All of the woodpeckers will regularly visit these sites. In addition, the limbs and trunks will endlessly be searched over by chickadees, titmice, nuthatches, Brown Creeper, Bushtit, certain warblers, and other small birds that eat insects.

Dead trees also become valuable "condominium units" for birds, for many species of birds excavate nest holes in the slightly softened wood. It is not unusual to see a dead tree with 4 or 5 nest holes excavated in it, often quite near each other. Excavators include all of the woodpeckers and sapsuckers as well as chickadees and some nuthatches.

Once these holes are made, there are many other species that will reuse them. These include swallows, wrens, titmice, bluebirds, nuthatches, owls, flycatchers, American Kestrels, and many others. Think of these dead trees with excavated holes as natural birdhouses, for this is exactly what they are. Without them, all of the birds who use them would have no place to nest.

Another use of dead trees is that they are great places to see birds. Birds cannot seem to resist stopping and perching in them. We used to have a dead elm in the middle of our field, and we saw so many species because the birds landed there in full view.

Of course, some consideration for safety and appearance must also be taken. Dead limbs and dead trees should be left only where they will not endanger people or be a nuisance to neighbors.

Reuse Your Christmas Tree

After Christmas, you can make a present of your Christmas tree to the birds. After removing all ornaments, lights, and tinsel from the tree, take it outside and stand it up a few feet from your bird feeders. The birds will love it and use it to perch on before and after going to the feeder; they will also use it for cover during rain or snow.

You can add to the attractiveness and usefulness of the tree by decorating it with foods birds will eat. Some people make chains of popcorn or cranberries with string and a needle and drape these over the tree. Other people take opened pinecones and press suet or peanut butter between the scales, then roll them in bird seed and hang them off the tree. This is a nice way to celebrate the season with your backyard birds.

Leave Leaves Alone

Here is something to do that will actually save you time and energy in your gardening chores. Don't rake up the leaves.

Obviously, you may want to rake them up off your lawn and driveway so they will not kill the grass or make the pavement slippery. But if fallen leaves gather under shrubs or in a wooded area

You can use a suet holder to offer nesting material for birds. This one is filled with fur combed from a golden retriever, and it attracts chickadees and titmice.

where there is no grass, then you can attract more birds by leaving them there.

Fallen leaves provide nutrients to the soil as they decay and, as they accumulate, form an insulating layer over the soil that keeps it warmer and moister. Insects and other soil animals thrive under these conditions.

There are many garden birds that love to feed where there are fallen leaves, including thrushes, thrashers, towhees, and many sparrows. In our garden we have many woodsy areas where we let leaves accumulate, especially under rhododendrons near our feeders. Species that regularly feed there are Eastern Towhee, Northern Cardinal, Brown Thrasher, and, during migration, Swainson's and Hermit Thrushes and White-throated and Fox Sparrows.

Create a Dust Bath

The notion of bathing in dust may seem a little contradictory to us, but it works just fine for birds. Birds go to dusty spots, nestle down in the dust, fluff out their feathers, and rapidly flutter. This action infiltrates their feathers with dust, which is then shaken out. After this the birds often preen.

The function of dust bathing is not exactly known, but it most likely helps birds rid their feathers of mites or other small feather parasites.

Create a dust bath by choosing a sunny area about three feet square near a feeder. Clear it of vegetation and hollow out the existing earth for 2–3 inches. Fill the hollow with fine dust, such as that found along the side of a dirt road. You can edge the dust bath area with small boards or stones to keep vegetation from growing back in.

We have a natural dusty site under the side of our garden shed and one year we had a group of nine Bobwhites almost every day walk single file over to the dusting area to use it.

House Sparrows in city areas often dust bathe near home plate on baseball diamonds.

Create a Hedgerow

A hedgerow is a long line of shrubs and small trees at the border of a field or lawn. It is a superb place for birds at all seasons, providing food, shelter, and nesting sites.

If you leave the leaves on the ground instead of raking them up, birds like this Brown Thrasher will come and feed on the seeds and insects beneath them.

Places to plant a hedgerow are along a sunny boundary between two properties, at the edge of a field, or in an open area you want to divide. Plant it with any of the berry-producing shrubs listed in the chapter Shrubs That Attract Birds. You can also plant some of the smaller trees such as hackberry, mulberry, or mountain ash. Over the years, you may need to cut back invasive trees or shrubs that do not produce food for birds.

We have a long hedgerow at the edge of a field. It contains blackberry, highbush cranberry, gray-stemmed dogwood, eastern red cedar, mountain ash, and a mulberry tree. We also have invasive black locust and buckthorn trees that we periodically cut out of the hedgerow. The blackberries try to spread out into the field, but we control them by mowing off their shoots when we mow the grass.

Our hedgerow is heavily used by nesting, wintering, and migrant birds. Brown Thrashers, Gray Catbirds, Common Yellowthroats, and Song Sparrows nest there. House Finches, Northern Cardinals, Cedar Waxwings, and Dark-eyed Juncos feed there all winter, and during migration we have had Mourning, Black-and-white, and Yellow-rumped Warblers, Lincoln's Sparrows, and Swainson's Thrushes stop by.

Provide Nesting Material in Spring

Birds need to find nesting material when they start building in spring. You can help them by providing certain materials that they often use. These materials include short pieces of string (6 inches or less), hair, fur from dogs, dry grass, pine needles, bark strips (from grape, birch, or weed stalks). Place these materials in an open-mesh container and hang the container somewhere in the open where birds frequent.

You can buy nesting material in bird specialty stores or you can make your own. We place the fur from our dog in a wire-mesh suet holder and hang it from the lower limb of a tree. Chickadees and titmice are very attracted to it and take such large mouthfuls that they can barely fly off. We get the fun of seeing them and we also can follow them with our binoculars to where they are nesting.

We provide pine needles for our bluebirds by placing the material on the ground near the nest boxes, and we provide chicken feathers for our Tree Swallows in the same way or by just throwing them in the air when the swallows are near — they gather them in midair.

"Bird-Friendly" Lawns and Lawn Alternatives

What Good Are Lawns?

Lawn areas can be attractive to many species of birds; however, they are only one part of a multidimensional environment that birds need. Lawns provide open areas where birds can safely look for seeds, insects, and earthworms, as well as other invertebrates. Birds that use lawns include doves, thrushes (including of course robins), sparrows, grackles, mockingbirds, catbirds, crows, geese, some

In spring through fall, bluebirds feed mainly on insects that they collect from short-grass areas such as lawns. If you apply chemicals to kill weeds or insects in your lawn, it is very likely that you will harm the birds that feed there, such as this male Western Bluebird.

ducks, and flickers. Bluebirds also particularly favor short-grass areas, for they typically sit on a perch, look for insects below, then dive down to get the insects and fly back to their perch. We keep mowed areas around our bluebird houses, and this is one of the reasons they nest on our property.

But lawns are only good for birds if they are healthy, contain diverse plants, and are free of pesticides. In this chapter, we will give you many tips to making your lawn areas "bird-friendly."

How to Make Your Lawn Healthier

There are many ways to improve the health of your lawn and many reasons for doing so — you'll spend less time caring for it and less money trying to keep it green, and you'll get more enjoyment from its greenery, more enjoyment from the birds that come to it, and a sense of well-being that comes from knowing you are helping, rather than harming, the environment.

Mowing Practices

The first four tips have to do with mowing. Set your mower to the highest setting that is right for your type of grass; this is 2 1/2–3 inches for most grasses in the Northeast and upper Midwest (see the books listed in Resources for mowing heights of other grasses). Taller grass conserves moisture, encourages root growth and new grass shoots, produces more food for the plant, and creates a richer environment for insects and invertebrates that birds might like.

Next, keep your mower blade sharp. You can tell if it is sharp by looking at the tops of your grass blades after mowing. If they are all frayed, then it is dull; if they are cleanly cut off, then it is sharp. Cleanly cut grass reduces the loss of moisture in the

American Robins are another bird that often feeds on lawns. Chemical fertilizers can change the acidity of your lawn so that earthworms no longer want to live there. Using organic fertilizer creates a good soil for earthworms and will make your lawn bird-friendly.

grass and helps prevent the entrance of diseases into the plant.

Third, use a mower that automatically mulches the cut grass pieces by chopping them up. This is not only easier, for you do not have to haul away the clippings, but it also continually enriches the soil of your lawn as these tiny clippings decompose. Grass clippings do not create thatch; if they are short, they start to decompose within one week and feed nitrogen back to the grass by the second week.

And the last tip is to mow your grass only when it needs it, rather than on a particular day of the week. You should not cut off more than 1/3 the length of the grass. More frequent, shorter mowings encourage more root growth.

Creating Good Soil

The next tips concern the health of the soil under your lawn. Your lawn is only as good as the soil beneath it. Healthy soil has the correct acidity (pH), organic nutrients, organisms that eat the grass clippings and thatch, and is airy, rather than compacted.

Check the acidity of your lawn soil with a little kit from your lawn and garden store. It should be a pH of 6–7. If it is more acid or more alkaline than this, then the grass will not be able to absorb the nutrients in the soil, no matter how much fertilizer you add, and the organisms that break down the clippings will not thrive.

Add organic nutrients to the soil, either through the use of an organic fertilizer and a spreader or by spreading a thin layer (3/8 inch) of compost over the lawn.

Chemical and synthetic fertilizers can actually harm the grass in the long run. While they give the grass a quick boost of green, they encourage surface root growth, which can lead to soil compaction, and they acidify the soil, making it inhospitable for earthworms and many other organisms that decompose grass clippings and thatch. Synthetic and chemical fertilizers have primarily soluble nitrogen, most of which quickly dissolves and leaches down through or runs off the soil, out of reach of the grass. Organic fertilizers have slower-acting nutrients that the grass gradually uses over a longer period of time and very little is lost into the water system.

Healthy soil is full of microorganisms, such as bacteria and fungi, and also full of larger invertebrates, especially earthworms. These living parts of the soil help break down thatch, grass clippings, and old roots into nutrients for the grass; they aerate the soil, helping decomposition to take place, the roots of grass to get the air they need, and water to penetrate and remain in the soil; and they enrich the soil with their own decomposition.

You can keep these little organisms happy by keeping your soil at a pH of 6–7, keeping the soil from compacting, and using organic fertilizers. You can add these organisms to your soil by top dressing with compost or a rich topsoil or through using an organic fertilizer that contains some of these organisms.

The final way to help your soil is to keep it from getting compacted. Compacted soil does not let air or water penetrate and reach the grass roots. This creates stressed and unhealthy grass and also discourages the presence of microorganisms and earthworms. If you have regular routes that you use across your lawn that get compacted through walking, consider making them a path of pebbles or stone. This saves you the trouble of trying to grow

This looks like ordinary grass, but is actually full of a wide variety of plants, including clover, dandelions, sorrel, yarrow, and other wildflowers. It is low maintenance and creates a varied habitat for insect and animal life on which birds can feed.

grass on those difficult spots, and channels people's movements onto the path and off the grass. The grass is beautiful, the path is easier to walk on, and you do not have an area of unhealthy lawn.

Choosing the Right Grass for the Right Location

There are two aspects of location to consider: your climate and the specific area on your property where you want lawn. There are many types of grass available and each area of the country is best suited to certain types. The main types of grasses in northern climates include rye grasses, fescues, and bluegrasses, and there are many types of each. In the South, the best grasses include Bermuda grass, bahai grass, blue gramagrass, buffalograss, carpetgrass, and zoysia grasses. (See Resources for picking the best grass for your area.)

In addition, there are special grasses available today that are more resistant to insects. They have a fungus that lives within them and makes them unpalatable to many lawn pests. This fungus is called an endophyte, and some grasses, such as rye grasses and fescues, can be bred with the fungus already in the seeds. We use endophytically treated grasses on our property and they are wonderful.

No Pesticides

If you want birds, then you should avoid the use of all pesticides that contain chemicals harmful to birds. Even though many of these pesticides have been approved by government agencies, you should know that most experts agree that testing has not been thorough enough and that many pesticide chemicals are strongly implicated as causing cancer and birth defects in humans, not to mention birds and smaller, more susceptible, animals.

Many pesticide chemicals are regularly used by lawn care agencies or can be bought at lawn and garden centers for individual application. But before you put any chemical or have anyone else put a chemical on your lawn, be sure that it is not dangerous to wildlife or you. (See Resources for books on pesticides and herbicides.) This is one of the most important things that you can do to keep birds safe and protect the health of your local environment.

Green and gold is a native wildflower that forms a beautiful ground cover and lawn alternative. In addition, the birds feed on the seeds that mature from the flower heads.

Lawn Alternatives

There are many ways to reduce the amount of lawn on your property and attract more birds at the same time. By doing this you are freed from the extra time spent maintaining your lawn and have more time to watch the birds that you have attracted.

One of the best ways to accomplish this is by planting ground covers that also produce berries. On our property, we use creeping junipers, bearberry, cotoneaster, and lowbush blueberries to fill in areas where lawn once was.

You can also plant shrubs valuable to birds in some area of your yard where you have trouble growing grass and then mulch underneath them to keep weeds from growing. These areas can be very attractive at the edges of lawns and are a great resource for the birds.

The Perfect Lawn

What is the perfect lawn? Some may think that the perfect lawn is like an unblemished golf green. Others may say that the perfect lawn is an artificial grass. Still others may say that the perfect lawn is one that you do not have to maintain.

We have many types of lawns on our property. We have one area of field that we mow for the bluebirds, and it contains all kinds of other plants besides grasses — dandelions, sorrel, plantain, daisies, wild carrot, and hawkweed, to mention just a few. This is our idea of the perfect lawn for the bluebirds and other birds that come to our field. It is rich in diversity, produces seeds of many kinds, has many different plants that different insects utilize, and we never fertilize, water, or weed it.

We have another area of grass that connects our house to the field and we have grown some tough fescues in here. They are fine-bladed and feel good on bare feet in summer. We fertilize them with an organic fertilizer once a year in fall, but we never water them, for they are fairly drought resistant.

And finally, we have a small area of grass near our perennial flower beds that we like to look like a carpet of green. We have planted some good perennial rye grasses there; we top dress the area with compost once a year and we weed it by hand. It is very small and easy to take the added care with. This is the perfect lawn for our smaller garden area.

So, be open to having various kinds of "perfect lawns" all over your property.

Good "Weeds"

What Is a Weed?

"Weed" is not a botanical category but a relative term. Some people say a weed is any plant growing where you do not want it to grow. Thus, even a rose might be called a weed if it were growing in the middle of your lawn. Many plants we call weeds in North America are valued in other parts of the world as foods or as beautiful plants in the flower garden.

But despite the fact that weediness is in the eye of the beholder, there are certain plants that continually grow where they are not wanted, and these plants tend to have at least three features in common. They are aggressive colonizers, either producing a lot of seeds or spreading through rhizomes or runners. They grow primarily on ground that has been recently disturbed and dug up by either humans, other animals, or a natural occurrence such as a flood or fire. And most are widespread in North America and not native to this continent but were brought here by early settlers from Europe, either knowingly, as herbs, or accidentally, as in livestock feed or in the ballast of ships.

How Can Weeds Be Good?

We were recently teaching a bird gardening course and a participant said, "I have a weedy area on my property and I do not know whether to get rid of it or leave it. How can I tell if the weeds are good for the birds?" The answer is that weeds can be good if they provide food or nesting areas for birds and they are not so aggressive that they crowd out native species of plants.

Many plants that we often call weeds fit these requirements. And most of them are good for birds because they produce seeds. These include most of the upland weeds and all the grasses. A few common weeds offer some other things for birds. Jewelweed provides nectar for the Ruby-throated Hummingbird in the East. Cattails provide roots and seeds for waterfowl, nesting supports for Red-winged Blackbirds, Yellow-headed Blackbirds, and Marsh Wrens, and cover for rails and other marsh

Good Weeds

Upland Weeds	Region
Annuals	
Filarees (*Erodium* spp.)	NW, SW
Goosefoot (*Chenopodium* spp.)	All
Jewelweed (*Impatiens* spp.)	NE, SE
Pigweed (*Amarantus* spp.)	All
Ragweed (*Ambrosia* spp.)	All
Smartweed (*Polygonum* spp.)	All
Sunflowers (*Helianthus* spp.)	All
Perennials	
Dandelion (*Taraxacum* spp.)	All
Pokeweed (*Phytolacca americana*)	All
Biennials	
Thistle (*Circium* spp.)	All
Grasses	
Foxtails (Bristlegrass) (*Setaria* spp.)	All
Panicgrasses (*Panicum* spp.)	All
Crabgrasses (*Digitaria* spp.)	All
Sedges (*Carex* spp.)	All
Water Plants	
Bulrushes (*Scirpus* spp.)	All
Smartweeds (*Polygonum* spp.)	All
Cattails (*Typhus* spp.)	All
Pondweeds (*Potamogeton* spp.)	All
Widgeongrass (*Ruppia maritima*)	All

Pokeweed should be encouraged on your property, for the birds love to eat the fruits that gradually mature throughout the last half of summer. It is a perennial and will continue to come up each year from the same spot.

Teasel, on the left, and mullein, on the right, are both "good" weeds. They both provide lots of seeds for birds, and mullein attracts many overwintering insects, which this male Downy Woodpecker is probably looking for.

birds. Thistles provide seeds and nesting material for goldfinches. And pondweed and widgeongrass provide food for most of our ducks that feed on vegetation in ponds and lakes.

Where to Find and Keep Weeds

There are many places on your property where weeds can be found. We have weeds at the edge of our property where we do not mow. Some of these areas could be mowed, but we try to leave them tall so that the weeds have a chance to produce seeds.

We also have an old garden bed that we have not tended, and it is full of weeds. The birds love it and it is a very productive area. The problem is that many of the best weeds growing there, such as ragweed and pigweed, are annuals, and in order to keep them growing each year, there needs to be bare earth. We now rototill that area each spring and then just let it go to seed with weeds. All fall and winter it is like a natural bird feeder that attracts lots of birds, including juncos and native sparrows.

Another place to let weeds grow can be your vegetable garden at the end of the season. After harvesting your vegetables, let the garden produce weed seeds all winter for the birds. You can mulch over them in the spring to prevent them from sprouting anew early in the season.

We also get weeds growing on bare earth around the property. These spots include compost piles, brush piles, delivered piles of loam, places where the snowplow has scraped away the grass, entrances to woodchuck dens, and molehills. Weeds grow in all of these places and they all attract birds.

In a wet marshy area of our field we let the plants grow undisturbed, and we get many weeds, like smartweed and bulrush, growing there.

We also have some large areas of lawn that are just mowed field grasses, and they contain various "weeds" or wildflowers, such as foxtail and dandelion. We periodically let these grow long during summer, allowing them to produce seeds, and then the birds to come feed.

If you have a pond, this is another important area to let good weeds grow. Pondweed and widgeongrass feed the ducks; cattails provide nesting spots and cover.

Invasive Exotics and Natural Natives

What Are Exotic or Native Species?

Native species are roughly defined as plants and animals that have naturally grown and reproduced over a long period of time in a given habitat. Exotics are plants and animals that were taken from one geographical area and introduced into a different geographical area as a result of human activity. To some extent, these terms are relative, for whether plants and animals are defined as native or exotic is always a result of a certain assumed time scale and geographical area.

Multiflora rose is imported from Asia, and in some areas of North America is invasive and crowds out native species. At the same time, birds, such as this Northern Cardinal, love to eat the berries and nest among its dense branching.

Is This an Important Distinction?

Certainly the history of life on earth has been one of continual movement of plants and animals into new areas and their eventual success or failure in those areas. But today, the movement of aggressive exotic species into new areas, as a result of human travel and commerce, has grown to such an extent that as a destroyer of natural habitats it is second only to destruction by humans.

Bioinvasion, as the introduction of aggressive exotic species is called, can adversely affect the environment in several ways. For example, on our property, a shrub called European buckthorn, *Rhamnus frangula,* has begun to grow in the understory of our woods. It grows densely, crowds out other native woodland shrubs, shades out native woodland wildflowers, and produces berries that birds eat. The understory of our woods has become, in a few spots, a monoculture of European buckthorn.

Now you might say that it could be seen as a good plant, for it produces berries that the birds eat; we also have seen hummingbirds take nectar from the flowers. The problem is that it reduces the diversity of other plants in our forests and this, in turn, will eventually reduce the diversity of the animals that can live there.

Not all exotic species are a problem. Some are introduced and continue to live in their new environment without taking over. The problem is with exotic species that, like European buckthorn, are also wildly successful in their new habitat. In its native habitat it is unlikely to have been dominant, but in the Northeast and Upper Midwest of North America, it is crowding out many native species.

The Southeast has many exotic plants, two of the most invasive are limited to Florida at the moment. They are Brazilian pepper, *Schinus tere-*

Invasive Exotics

Wildflowers and Weeds

Canada thistle (*Cirsium arvense*)

Crown vetch (*Coronilla varia*)

Garlic mustard (*Alliaria petiolata*)

Japanese knotweed (*Polygonum cuspidatum*)

Nodding thistle (*Carduus nutans*)

Purple loosestrife (*Lythrum salicaria*)

Spotted knapweed (*Centaurea maculosa*)

Water Plants

Water Hyacinth (*Eichhornia crassipes*)

Vines

Japanese honeysuckle (*Lonicera japonica*)

Kudzu (*Pueraria lobata*)

Oriental bittersweet (*Celastrus orbiculatus*)

Shrubs

Australian saltbush (*Atriplex semibaccata*)

Brazilian pepper (*Schinus terebinthifolius*)

Common buckthorn (*Rhamnus cathartica*)

Common privet (*Ligustrum vulgare*)

European buckthorn (*Rhamnus frangula*)

Japanese barberry (*Berberis thunbergii*)

Multiflora rose (*Rosa multiflora*)

Russian olive (*Elaeagnus angustifolia*)

Tartarian honeysuckle (*Lonicera tatarica*)

Winged euonymus (*Euonymus alatus*)

Trees

Norway maple (*Acer platanoides*)

Melaleuca (*Melaleuca quinquenervia*)

White mulberry (*Morus alba*)

---

binthifolius, and Melaleuca, *Melaleuca quinquenervia.* It has been suggested that these two plants are taking over native habitats in Florida faster than urban development by humans.

What Can We Do?

There are many things that each of us can do to help reduce the negative effects of plant bioinvasions. The first is to become aware of which plants are considered the most problematic, especially when it comes to attracting birds. Many of the most aggressive species are shrubs that produce berries; and they are in part successful because the birds eat the berries and disperse the seeds to new areas.

In the recent past, government agencies actually recommended these species as plantings to attract birds. They were good — too good. Now, there is a greater awareness of their overall, long-term effects. Many are still sold by nurseries, compounding the problem. We have provided a chart of the species that are considered by many to be most invasive and aggressive and that you might be tempted to use to attract birds.

Try to avoid buying and planting these species on your property. If you already have them growing on your property, then try to reduce their numbers gradually or eliminate them altogether. In the case of shrubs, you can either dig them out, cut them down to the ground and then repeatedly mow over the area, or cut them down and paint the tops of the stems with an environmentally safe herbicide.

Also, you can teach others about the effects on our native habitats of invasive exotic plants.

Tartarian honeysuckle is one of many shrub honeysuckles imported from Eurasia. It is widespread because birds eat the fruits, fly to new areas, and void the seeds in their droppings. This male American Goldfinch will probably not eat these berries, for it prefers seeds.

Bird Feeders

One of the Best Ways to Attract Birds

Bird feeders that offer a variety of seeds are an essential part of any bird garden. They attract a wide range of birds to your property, where the birds will then be able to take advantage of all of your other plantings.

Consistent use of bird feeders throughout the year and over several years will attract increasingly more birds. Birds become familiar with your feeder

This feeder offers both safflower and sunflower seeds and has attracted a male Red-bellied Woodpecker (left) and a male Northern Cardinal (right).

setup and will fly longer distances to visit. Also, birds on migration will find it and stop each year on their way north or south.

Another benefit of feeders is that birds attract other birds. All birds watch other birds to see where they are feeding in the hopes that they will discover food for themselves. We are convinced that, on our property, we attract other species that do not even use the feeders, simply because of all of the activity around our feeders.

Seeds Versus Fruits

Many of the plants in a bird garden produce fruits. Few garden plants produce seeds in the quantities needed to attract certain birds — unless you can plant a field of barley or oats. Feeders attract seed-eating birds, while most plantings attract fruit-eating birds. Thus, feeders along with plantings attract the greatest number and variety of birds.

Best Basic Setup

The feeder setup that will attract the most birds will offer four basic foods: sunflower seed, mixed seed, thistle seed, and suet. For information on hummingbird feeders see the chapter Creating a Hummingbird Garden.

Sunflower Seed — More birds are attracted to sunflower than to any other type of seed. Sunflower seed should be offered to birds in either a tubular feeder or a hopper-type feeder. These feeders can be hung or mounted on poles. Since birds really love sunflower, it is best to get a feeder that will hold 2 or more quarts of seed and is easy to fill.

Sunflower seed is available in two basic types:

Feeders create a great opportunity to see bird behavior. Here is mate-feeding between Northern Cardinals. During courtship and early breeding stages, the male brings food to the female.

striped sunflower seed, which has gray and white longitudinal stripes; and black oil sunflower seed, which is smaller and all black. You can buy sunflower seed with the hulls on or removed. Buying hulled sunflower seed has many advantages. It is more concentrated, so you will not need to carry and store as many bags, and it is less messy around the feeder, for the birds eat all of the seed and do not leave the hulls behind.

All studies show that birds prefer black oil sunflower seed and hulled sunflower seed over striped sunflower seed.

Mixed Seed — Mixed seed includes a variety of seeds birds love, such as cracked corn, white and red proso millet, peanut hearts, and safflower seeds. Mixed seed should be scattered on the open ground under other feeders or be placed on an open tray near the ground. Birds that usually feed on the ground, such as sparrows, juncos, doves, and Northern Cardinals, will eat mixed seed. Some mixed seed has sunflower seed in it, in varying proportions. This is a good idea, for it makes it even more attractive.

Thistle — Thistle seed (also called Niger seed, which is its true name) is a small black seed that is a favorite of goldfinches, Pine Siskins, and other finches. Thistle should be placed in a tubular thistle feeder that is mounted on a pole or hung. A thistle feeder has tiny holes small enough to keep the seed from spilling out, but large enough to let the birds peck at it.

Suet — The last element to a successful feeder setup is suet. This is a special fat found near the kidneys of cattle. You can ask for suet at your local supermarket meat counter, or you can buy already-made suet cakes.

Suet cakes have many advantages over straight suet. First of all they have been melted down and solidified two or more times. This makes them less likely to melt and they will not go rancid, as raw suet might. Suet cakes are also made today with many added ingredients, such as peanut hearts and berries. You can test these out and see which types your birds like best. Another advantage to suet cakes is that they come in blocks that fit neatly into suet holders that are made of coated wire mesh.

Suet holders can be attached to tree trunks near your other feeders or hung near other feeders. Some hopper-type feeders actually have places to put suet cakes at either end.

When to Start and Stop Feeding

The answer to this is easy — start now and never stop. Feeding birds is delightful to do throughout the year and birds always need our help. We keep all four types of feeders going all year on our property. We have year-round residents that we see all the time, we have spring and fall migrants that come to fuel up on their journey, and we get summer-breeding birds who need extra help during the difficult time of breeding and who bring their young to the feeder from mid- to late summer.

Some people worry that birds will get too dependent on feeders, that they will get "lazy," or that they will get fat and not be able to fly. None of these are true. Other people worry that if they go away for a week or two and their feeders become empty, the birds will suffer. In truth, although wild birds will miss your feeder, they always feed in the wild as well, and will find other sources of food. When we go away, we just hire a local youngster to fill our feeders once a week. Kids love earning some extra money and it introduces them to bird feeding.

Where to Place Feeders

It is best to have your feeder setup near some small trees or large shrubs where the birds can land and perch before going to the feeders, or where they can dive for cover in the case of danger.

We have one of our feeder setups near a stand of rhododendrons. The birds seem to like the year-round cover and they often wait within the bushes before venturing out to feed on the ground. When something scares them, they dart back into the bushes.

Be sure to put up feeders where you can see

This is a nice feeder setup with thistle, suet, peanuts, and sunflower offered from aboveground feeders, and mixed seed scattered on the ground and on a tray. The rhododendrons behind the feeders are superb as shelter and cover for the visiting birds.

them from inside your house. This will give you the maximum enjoyment from the birds that visit. We have our feeders outside our kitchen table window and we have another set of feeders outside our office windows.

One of our favorite activities is sitting at our kitchen table and watching the bird activity at our feeders on a winter day; or on an early-summer morning with the windows open, hearing bird songs and seeing Rose-breasted Grosbeaks flying down to our sunflower seed feeder and male Northern Cardinals feeding seeds to the females as part of courtship.

Feeders are there to help the birds, but they are also a wonderful way to bring the exciting lives of birds nearer to your home and family.

Cleaning Feeders

Over the months feeders and feeder areas can get messy with uneaten seeds, hulls from eaten seeds, and bird droppings. It is best to clean the area beneath the feeders every month or so. It is also good to clean the feeders themselves every few months. Not only will your feeder area look better, but it will be safer for the birds.

Oh Yes, What About Squirrels?

Over the years we have become convinced that there are two types of people in the world of bird feeding: those that want to keep squirrels off their feeders and those that want to continually match wits with squirrels. If you want to do the latter, then be our guest, but remember that the squirrel has 24 hours a day to think of ways to foil you.

If you want to keep squirrels off your above-ground feeders, this can be easily done. First of all, place your feeders 8 feet away from any support from which a squirrel could jump to them. Second, mount your feeders on thin metal poles available at any bird feeder store. Third, place a stovepipe baffle, 2 feet long and 6 inches in diameter, over the supporting pole and just under the feeder. Squirrels will try to crawl up the pole and will end up inside the stovepipe.

This male Northern Flicker is feeding on suet mixed with seeds.

This actually works 90–95 percent of the time. We have many feeders and many squirrels, but rarely do we have squirrels on our feeders.

In addition to this, we let the squirrels feed to their heart's delight on the mixed seed that we scatter on the ground. This keeps them and the chipmunks busy and takes their minds off the aboveground feeders, where our more expensive seed is housed.

Birdhouses

Add Beauty and Homes to Your Garden

Birdhouses are fun, picturesque, and can make a property or garden instantly look like your own private bird sanctuary.

Birdhouses are now available everywhere. In addition to being used to attract birds, they are also used as home decorations, sold as antiques, and even bought as collectors' items. But remember, when you are trying to attract birds, it is important that the house be functional and safe for the birds. To be sure of this, see What Makes a Good Birdhouse?

This female Northern Flicker is living in a homemade birdhouse created from a hollowed-out aspen trunk placed on a telephone pole. Most woodpeckers excavate their own cavities, but flickers occasionally use preexisting ones.

Do Birds Need Birdhouses?

The answer is yes. Birdhouses are additional nest sites for birds that nest in natural cavities. There are 86 species of North American birds that nest in tree cavities. Some, such as the woodpeckers, can excavate their own holes in trees, but the majority cannot — they depend on finding holes.

As we cut down trees for development and wood, we take away homes for these cavity nesters. When we add birdhouses, we add homes for birds.

Many of our best-loved garden birds nest in tree holes and, therefore, love birdhouses. They include chickadees, titmice, nuthatches, tree swallows, wrens, and bluebirds. By putting up good birdhouses, you can have these birds nesting in your garden and on your property.

Will Any Bird Use a Birdhouse?

Each species of bird tends to have a favorite location for its nests. Some birds, like pheasants and quail, nest only on the ground. Birds such as mockingbirds and thrashers nest mostly in shrubs. Others, such as tanagers and vireos, nest mostly on tree branches. Others nest only in tree cavities.

Each species is quite specific as to its nesting habits and does not vary. Therefore, you will not find any of the cavity nesters, such as bluebirds, making an open, cuplike nest in a shrub; nor will you find any of the birds that make open nests, such as Northern Cardinals, ever using a birdhouse.

What Makes a Good Birdhouse?

A good birdhouse is one that provides a safe and protected place for the birds to raise their young. Here are its main features.

This is another hollowed-out log with a base and a roof that a Tree Swallow is using as a nesting cavity. Tree Swallows are dependent upon finding cavities that are naturally formed or created by other birds, such as woodpeckers.

It should be made of wood. Wood naturally insulates the birds from the heat of the day and the cool temperatures at night. Wood birdhouses can be painted or stained on the outside, but not on the inside, for it may harm the birds.

To accommodate most garden birds, it should have an entrance hole that is 1 1/2 inches in diameter; a smaller hole will exclude many species. The entrance hole should also be at least 6 inches above the floor of the box. This is because the birds have to build a nest in the bottom of the box. Also, you do not want the eggs or young to fall out or be subject to predators reaching directly into the entrance hole.

The inside dimensions of the box need to be about 5 by 5 inches in order to leave enough room for the eggs and the young to develop and not be overcrowded.

There should be a roof overhang that keeps the rain out of the entrance hole and drainage holes in the bottom of the box in case water gets in.

There should also be ventilation holes or a ventilation slit near the top of the box to help cool it during hot weather.

Check to be sure that there is an easy way to open the box, either through a top opening or a side or front opening. This will enable you to monitor the development of the young and clean out the box at the end of the season.

Finally, you need a way to hang the box or attach it to a tree or post.

If these basic criteria are met, then the actual design of the birdhouse can be as simple as an unpainted wood box or as elaborate as a miniature Swiss chalet with flowers painted on the balcony. In general, the birds are just looking for the right size cavity in the right location; the rest of the box is more for our benefit and sense of taste than theirs.

Birdhouses should have only one compartment and one entrance hole. The condominium or apartment house look is only suitable for Purple Martins, and they need houses with entirely different dimensions and construction criteria. See Resources for more on Purple Martin housing.

Where to Put Up Your Birdhouse

Different species of birds prefer different habitats. Which habitat you place a house in will in some part determine which birds you attract.

Placing a birdhouse in an open area like a garden, field, or large lawn will be most attractive to swallows, bluebirds, European Starling, and House Sparrow. A birdhouse placed at the edge of woods will attract chickadees, wrens, European Starling, and House Sparrow. Birdhouses placed in woods will attract chickadees, titmice, nuthatches, and woodpeckers.

Most houses should be placed about 30 feet from continuous pedestrian activity, although a house in the middle of a vegetable garden will be readily accepted by House Wrens or Tree Swallows. Do not place birdhouses near roads, for the birds might be hit by cars as they fly back and forth.

Most birds will nest in birdhouses placed 4–6 feet high, a height that enables most people to monitor the nests easily and clean out the box at the end of the year. Houses can be higher and the birds will accept them.

Which compass direction the birdhouse faces makes little difference, although facing the entrance East or Southeast lets in early-morning sun to warm it up after a cool night and also protects the inside from hot late-afternoon sun. In general, try to face a birdhouse in such a way that the birds have ample room to fly to and from the entrance hole.

You can put up as many birdhouses as you want.

Welcome the birds to your backyard with birdhouses. Decorating birdhouses is fun and, as long as there is no paint inside, does not harm the birds.

Birdhouses come in a variety of shapes and sizes. All of these houses are suitable for chickadees, titmice, wrens, swallows, and bluebirds.

Birdhouses in open fields are attractive to Tree Swallows and bluebirds.

On about 3 acres of our property we have 20 birdhouses. Not all are used each year. In fact, we rarely know which ones will be used, for it changes from year to year. If a birdhouse is not used for 2 years, we move it to see if a bird will find the new location more attractive.

Monitoring Your Nesting Birds

Once you have begun to see birds leave and enter your birdhouse, you can have the fun of monitoring the nest. This involves walking carefully up to the birdhouse when you think the bird has left and slowly opening the side or top. Look briefly inside to see what is there and then close it up and walk away.

Keep a record of what you see. Is there a nest? Are there eggs? If so, how many and what color? Are there hatched young? If you do this every 3–4 days, you will not only have the fun of watching the progress of the birds, but you may also be able to help the birds by removing eggs that did not hatch or young birds that may die. The only way really to know if your birdhouse is working for the birds is to look in.

When the young are about 10 days old, it is best to stop opening the nest or they might leave the nest prematurely.

Contrary to popular myths, touching birdhouses or nests will not scare away the birds, nor will opening up the birdhouse blind the baby birds. Monitoring is done by all responsible birdhouse owners.

Predators and Unwanted Guests

There are several mammals and a few snakes that may prey on the occupants of your birdhouses. But you can protect your birds from these predators. The easiest way is to mount your birdhouse on a pole after placing a 4-foot length of PVC pipe, 4 inches in diameter, over the base of the pole. This portion of pipe can also be hung on the pole beneath the birdhouse. This will keep most predators from getting to the birds.

Two species of birds that were imported to North America in the 1800s, the House Sparrow and the European Starling, live in tree cavities and are aggressive competitors with our native birds who need these sites to reproduce.

In some cases, these birds can come into a birdhouse and kill the owner and/or young and then take over the site. European Starlings are a little larger than most of our garden birds that use birdhouses. A 1 1/2-inch-diameter nest hole is too small for European Starlings to enter, but just large enough for all of our cavity-nesting garden birds.

House Sparrows are more difficult to control since they are smaller and can get into a 1 1/2-inch-diameter nest hole. One way to discourage them is to continually remove their nesting material every 2 days. This may make them move elsewhere and make your birdhouse available to native birds. The nests of native birds are protected by federal law, but those of introduced birds, such as the European Starling and House Sparrow are not.

Territories and Birdhouse Spacing

Most birds have territories during breeding. This is an area around the nest site that is defended against all other birds of the same species. A territory is not necessarily the whole area that a bird lives in, just the area that it defends from others of its species. House Wrens tend to stay within their territories (about 1/4 acre); Tree Swallows roam widely and defend just the area right around the nest site (about 10 feet in diameter).

Bluebirds have territories of about 2–3 acres. Thus, if you have 2 birdhouses within 100 feet of each other, whatever bluebird occupies one of these birdhouses first will probably chase away any other bluebird that tries to nest in the second box. However, any other species of bird can nest in that open box, such as a House Wren, Tree Swallow, or Violet-green Swallow.

Birdhouses enable you to see the breeding behavior of birds up close. This male Eastern Bluebird is delivering an insect to its mate, who is inside the birdhouse, incubating the eggs.

Checklist for a Good Birdhouse

Made of wood
1 1/2-inch entrance hole
Entrance hole 6 inches above floor
Inside dimensions 5 by 5 inches
Roof overhang
Drainage holes
Ventilation holes
Easy way to open
Way to attach to a support

Territory Size of Common Birdhouse Birds

Species	Breeding Territory Size
Bluebirds	2–3 acres
Chickadees	8–10 acres
Nuthatches	20–30 acres
Swallows	10 feet around nest site
Wrens	1/4–1/2 acre

Birdbaths, Ponds, and Pools

Water — Essential for Birds and Beautiful for Gardens

Water is one of the four basic features to offer birds in your garden. Water is also one of the key features of a beautiful garden. Because of this double benefit it is always a successful addition.

We have already discussed why water is needed by birds, but let's take a moment here to discuss

Birds need water every day. Here, two Common Ground-Doves and a Mourning Dove are drinking together. Doves can sip water up through their bill. Most birds have to tilt their head back to drink the water they collect in their bill.

why it is such a great addition to a garden, regardless of the birds.

Water, whether it be in a small birdbath or in a large pond, provides reflections and, when the wind blows, movement on its surface. This can be a very living and shimmering element in a garden that is all composed of greenery and flower colors. Reflections double the number of flowers near it and reflect clouds and blue sky.

Water in containers such as whiskey barrels, large pots, or cisterns can also be a place to plant water plants such as rushes, water lilies, iris, and floating plants like water hyacinth.

And finally, water is a place where you can have a small recirculating fountain to create the sound of falling water. This sound can be a tremendous addition to the sensations of a garden, making it seem peaceful, idyllic, and even cooler on a warm, still summer day.

We have a lead English cistern in one of our flower beds with a small fountain. We grow water plants in it and place lush plants around it. People are always drawn to it even though it is small, and almost everybody who visits our garden comments on the calming quality of the water sound. One guest said that, after taking a book out to our garden to read, and hearing the water sound, he was so relaxed he went right to sleep.

Creating a Good Birdbath

There are many ways to create a birdbath, from as simple as a trash-can lid turned upside down to as complex as a flowing stream with waterfalls and pools. In all examples, though, there are certain requirements to meet to be sure that the bath will be useful for and attractive to the birds.

Most of the smaller garden birds bathe by using very shallow water, sometimes only about 1/2

Birdbaths can be beautiful structures within your garden plan.

inch deep. Often, they do not even get all the way in the water, but just stand at the edge and splash water on their bodies with a rapid motion of their bill.

Therefore, any birdbath that you create must have shallow areas near the edge that the birds can gradually step into. If your birdbath is about 1–2 inches deep, you can create shallow areas in it by placing a few thin, flat rocks around the edge that are submerged to varying depths. This gives the birds choices. If you have a larger pond or even a small artificial stream, be sure that smaller, safe, shallow areas exist where the birds can approach the water for bathing and drinking.

When larger birds, such as grackles, robins, or bluebirds, come to bathe, they need deeper water and seem to really like to get into it, splashing about. Therefore, you will also want some water that is about 2 inches deep in your bird bathing areas.

You will also need a way to clean your birdbath, for after a few visits by birds, there may be feathers and possibly droppings in and around the bath. We use a little scrub brush to swoosh out the old water each time we refill it. Water tends to evaporate

quickly from birdbaths, and the birds also splash it out as they bathe, so you will need to refill your birdbaths every 2–3 days.

Where to Place Your Birdbath

The bath should be placed in an area that appeals to the birds and where they already come. Baths can be near feeders if the seed does not fall into them. They can also be in gardens.

It is best to have shrubs and/or small trees near the bath, for this will be a place the birds can perch as they approach the bath to see that it is safe from predators and also a place to perch after the bath to preen and dry off.

If you have cats in the area, then you may want to have the birdbath more out in the open with no shrubbery immediately nearby. This makes it hard for a cat, that may hide in shrubbery, to catch the birds by surprise.

We place our birdbaths at different heights. We have one in a hollowed-out rock that is sunk into the ground, and the birds seem to like this one the most. We have others that are 6 inches off the ground and others that are 2–3 feet high.

It is important to note that the tops of many traditional birdbaths are heavy and unsteady. Small children may be tempted to reach up and pull on the bath top and it might fall. If small children will be visiting your garden, either have the birdbath out of reach or use one with a top that is sturdily attached.

Offering Water in Winter

Birds need water in winter as much as in summer. In some cases, they may need it even more, for many of the natural sources of water may be frozen and unavailable to them. Some birds eat snow and break pieces of icicles for water in cold climates.

Once we saw a whole flock of Cedar Waxwings flying out and back from their perches on a willow during a snowstorm. They looked like they were catching insects, but when we looked through our binoculars, we saw that they were catching snowflakes.

If you live in a warmer climate, keep water out all year. If you live in a colder climate and there are

times when the temperature drops below freezing, then you will need a way to keep the water melted. The best way to do this is through the use of small heating elements that can be plugged in and then warm the water to above freezing. Some birds even bathe in winter.

Water Sound: A Magic Attractant

Few things attract birds more readily than the sound of dripping or trickling water. If there is a way to add this sound to your birdbath, then by all means do so. Birds obviously hear the sound and seem to be irresistibly drawn to it. This is particularly true in spring and fall, when migrating birds must locate water to help fuel them on their journey, and may rely on the sound of water to locate it more quickly in areas with which they are unfamiliar.

For decades, bird photographers have known this and always set up good drip fountains to attract birds to spots where they have a camera all ready to get a picture.

Water sound is also particularly effective in

You can also create little pools in your garden. This one has running water, the sound of which is a strong attractant to many birds.

Here is a chance meeting between a male Painted Bunting, on the left, and a female Northern Cardinal, on the right. This shallow, natural pool is perfect for small birds to bathe in.

You can attract birds to your deck with a small birdbath. Here is a male American Robin about to take a drink.

It is fun to watch birds bathe. Each species does it a little differently. This male Northern Cardinal is really making the water fly.

attracting birds in desert areas, where water may be an even greater attraction than food.

There are several ways to create water sound. You can use a little recirculating water pump connected to a fountain or bubbler in the center of your birdbath; or you can create a stream with the recirculating pump carrying the water to the top of one rock where it flows over the rock and drips into another pool.

Some people just take a plastic jug and poke a fine hole in the bottom and suspend the jug over the birdbath to create a slow drip sound. Once, in the Southwest, we were in a high mountain canyon where there was a campground. A pipe had been attached to a spring and was dripping water on rocks. There was a Painted Redstart that could not resist the sound and stayed in the area of the dripping throughout the hour that we were there.

How to Make Ponds and Pools

Ponds and pools are wonderful additions to bird gardens, for they are larger than birdbaths, creating more reflection area and providing room for water plantings.

There are several ways to make these larger ponds. One is to excavate a shallow pond area, place a smooth layer of sand over the bottom, then line it with thick black plastic, available at most lawn and garden stores. Then place flat rocks around the edge of the pond to hide the plastic and put a few water-loving plants among the rocks for a naturalistic effect.

Another way is to excavate a deeper hole, smooth it out with sand, and buy a preformed black plastic pool to go into the hole. These come in all shapes and sizes, some rounded and some square. They are usually 1–3 feet deep and often have ledges around the edge to place pots of aquatic plants.

If you cannot or do not want to excavate a hole, you can use the squared preformed plastic pools aboveground by building a small frame out of wood to support the lip of the pool. Then you can cover the outside of the frame with siding. This can be quite pretty and the frame can be wide enough to provide a seating area around the edge of the pool.

If you make a pond or pool, the birds may be able to drink from it, but they will not be able to use it for bathing unless you create a shallow area where they can step in. This can be done by building up some large flat rocks at the edge or in the center of the pool.

Basic Birding Skills

Three Tips for Starting the Hobby

Birdwatching is a very popular hobby. Almost one out of every three Americans watches wild birds in some way, either at the bird feeder, in the backyard, or by taking trips into surrounding areas. The three tools we suggest that you have to start the hobby are binoculars, an easy-to-use field guide, and bird feeders (if you have a place to put them). Bird feeders bring the birds to you, binoculars help you see them up close, and field guides help you identify the birds and learn about their lives.

Binoculars are key to the hobby of bird watching. If possible, everybody in the family should have his or her own pair.

We have covered bird feeders in another chapter in this book. For an easy-to-use field guide, we recommend Stokes Field Guide to Birds: Eastern Region (or Western Region) or Stokes Beginner's Guide to Birds: Eastern Region (or Western Region). These are photographic guides with many helpful features to aid the beginning and intermediate birdwatcher, and they also contain complete information on the lives and behavior of the birds.

Binoculars for Everyone

We cannot emphasize enough how important it is to get a good pair of binoculars for everyone in your house who is interested. Also, when going to look at birds, *always* take binoculars. Binoculars bring birds up close, helping you see their beauty and behavior and getting you close enough that you can identify them. Here are a few tips about binoculars that will help you get a pair that work for you at the right price and the right quality.

Two Important Numbers — All binoculars are shown with 2 main numbers, for example, 7 x 35 or 8.5 x 42.

The first number refers to the power of the binoculars to magnify an object, in this case by 7 times or 8.5 times. It is best to get binoculars with magnification somewhere from 7 to 8.5. If you have binoculars more powerful than this, you may have trouble holding the image steady; any less powerful and you will not see the birds close enough to easily identify them.

The second number refers to the size, in millimeters, of the opening at the far end of the binoculars. The larger the opening, the more light is let through and the clearer you will see the bird. An opening size somewhere between 35 and 42 is good for most purposes.

A good way to look for birds is to sit for a while in one spot. Sometimes, when you become still, the birds accept you and become more active nearby. This can lead to seeing some special and exciting bird behavior.

Size and Weight — One of the mistakes many beginners make is choosing very light and very small binoculars, so they can easily take them on hikes and keep them in their pocket.

Unfortunately, very light and very small binoculars rarely have the power or let in enough light to be good for birdwatching. A good pair of birdwatching binoculars will probably not fit in your pocket and will weigh about 20–28 ounces.

Buy binoculars at a store that carries several brands so that you can try them all out. Get advice from other people who have binoculars and try looking through their different pairs.

If you enjoy birdwatching, it is worthwhile to invest in some good binoculars. They will help you see the birds for the rest of your life, resulting in your experiencing a tremendous amount of beauty and joy.

Where and When to Look for Birds

If you can set up feeders, start by looking at your feeder birds. Use binoculars when looking at them to see the details of their colors and shape. Next, venture outside to your yard. Depending on the season, you will see varying amounts of bird activity.

In spring, birds are most obviously active and making sounds because they are migrating, setting up territories, mating, building nests, and raising young. In summer, things get a little quieter; in early summer parents are feeding their nestlings and fledglings, and in late summer it is rather quiet, for most birds are less active and molting their feathers. In fall, many birds start to migrate south and there are greater numbers of birds than at any other time of year. In winter, there are just the resident or wintering birds, and a good place to watch many of these is at your feeder.

In spring and summer, be sure to take some time to sit in your yard for about an hour in the morning and just look closely at what your birds are doing. We guarantee you will see something new and exciting each time.

The Birds

Here are 103 species of birds that are common and can be attracted to your property. We have described their habitat, feeding, and nesting needs so that you can provide these essentials to attract the various species. Birds with similar needs are grouped together.

American Kestrel (female)
Habitat: Wide variety of open habitats, including urban areas.
Food: Voles, mice, birds, and insects; hovers and dives down to catch.
Nesting Needs: Needs large natural cavity in tree or birdhouse.

Screech-Owls (Eastern shown)
Habitat: Woods, swamps, parks, suburbs.
Food: Mice, insects, amphibians, birds.
Nesting Needs: Needs large natural cavity in tree or birdhouse; adds no lining.

Wood Duck (male and female)
Habitat: Wooded swamps, rivers.
Food: Aquatic plants, minnows, frogs.
Nesting Needs: Needs large natural cavity in tree or birdhouse; lined with wood chips and down.

Ring-necked Pheasant
(male and female)
Habitat: Farmlands with some woods or hedgerows.
Food: Waste grain, seeds, acorns, berries, insects; mixed seed on ground.
Nesting Needs: Nests on ground among tall grasses.

Northern Bobwhite
(male)
Habitat: Farmlands, brushy fields, open woodlands.
Food: Seeds, fruits, tender plant parts, insects; mixed seed on ground.
Nesting Needs: Nests on ground within 50 ft. of a clearing.

Gambel's Quail
(male)
Habitat: Arid scrubby areas, riverside woodlands.
Food: Seeds, tender plant parts, cacti fruit; mixed seed on ground.
Nesting Needs: Nests on ground near base of taller vegetation.

California Quail
Habitat: Open woodlands, shrubby areas, parks, gardens.
Food: Seeds, insects; mixed seed on ground.
Nesting Needs: Nests on ground near rock or log, sometimes in low tree.

Band-tailed Pigeon
Habitat: Dry pine forests inland, oaks along coast, parks, gardens.
Food: Seeds, acorns, berries; mixed seed at feeders.
Nesting Needs: Nests in trees on limb or in fork of branches.

Mourning Dove
(on nest with young)
Habitat: Almost any open habitat, including suburbs.
Food: Seeds and some insects; mixed seed on ground.
Nesting Needs: Nests on support of tree, shrub, cactus 3–30 ft. high.

Common Ground-Dove
Habitat: Open areas at edge of vegetation; suburbs.
Food: Seeds, insects, berries; mixed seed on ground.
Nesting Needs: Nests on ground in open area, beach, field, woods.

Ruby-throated Hummingbird
(male)
Habitat: Woods edges, streams, parks, gardens.
Food: Flower nectar, insects, spiders, tree sap; sugar water at feeders.
Nesting Needs: Nest of plant down and lichens on small limb of tree 10–20 ft. high.

Black-chinned Hummingbird
(male and female)
Habitat: Dry lowlands and foothills.
Food: Flower nectar, insects, spiders; sugar water at feeders.
Nesting Needs: Nest of plant down and lichens in tree or shrub 5–10 ft. high.

Anna's Hummingbird
(male)
Habitat: Open woods, shrubs, gardens, parks.
Food: Flower nectar, insects; sugar water at feeders.
Nesting Needs: Nest of plant down and lichens in tree or shrub 5–10 ft. high.

Broad-tailed Hummingbird (male)
Habitat: Open mountain woodlands and meadows.
Food: Flower nectar, insects, spiders, tree sap; sugar water at feeders.
Nesting Needs: Nest of plant down and lichens in tree or shrub 5–15 ft. high.

Rufous Hummingbird (male)
Habitat: Woods edges, thickets, parks, mountain meadows.
Food: Flower nectar, insects, spiders, tree sap; sugar water at feeders.
Nesting Needs: Nest of plant down and lichens in tree or shrub 5–15 ft. high.

Allen's Hummingbird (male)
Habitat: Woods, thickets, gardens, parks.
Food: Flower nectar, insects; sugar water at feeders.
Nesting Needs: Nest of plant down and lichens in vine or shrub.

Red-headed Woodpecker
Habitat: Farmlands, open woodlands, suburbs, orchards.
Food: Acorns, other nuts, insects under bark, tree sap, berries; suet at feeders.
Nesting Needs: Dead or live trees to excavate in.

Acorn Woodpecker
(male)
Habitat: Oak and pine woods, parks, suburbs.
Food: Mostly acorns cached in drilled holes, insects, tree sap; suet at feeders.
Nesting Needs: Dead or live trees to excavate in.

Red-bellied Woodpecker
(male)
Habitat: Woodlands, parks, suburbs.
Food: Insects under tree bark; suet, seeds, fruit at feeders.
Nesting Needs: Excavates hole in live wood, may use existing hole or birdhouse.

Nuttall's Woodpecker
(male)
Habitat: Shrublands, wooded streamsides, oak woods.
Food: Insects, fruit, berries; suet at feeders.
Nesting Needs: Standing dead wood to excavate in.

Downy Woodpecker
(male)
Habitat: Woods, farm-lands, suburbs.
Food: Insects under tree bark; suet and sunflower at feeders.
Nesting Needs: Standing dead wood to excavate in.

Hairy Woodpecker
(female)
Habitat: Woods, farm-lands, suburbs.
Food: Insects under tree bark; suet and sunflower at feeders.
Nesting Needs: Excavates nest in live wood.

Northern Flicker
(male)
Habitat: Parks, sub-urbs, farmlands, wood-lands.
Food: Ants on ground, catches insects in air, fruit; suet and seed at feeders.
Nesting Needs: Excavates usually in dead tree; may use existing hole or bird-house.

Pileated Woodpecker
(male)
Habitat: Mature forests, suburbs with large trees.
Food: Carpenter ants in large trees, insects, fruit; suet at feeders.
Nesting Needs: Excavates in dead wood 15–70 ft. high.

Western Wood-Pewee
Habitat: Open woods, streamside trees.
Food: Insects caught in the air.
Nesting Needs: Nest of plant down and fibers in tree 8–40 ft. high.

Black Phoebe
Habitat: Wooded streams and canyons, farms and suburbs near water.
Food: Insects in the air.
Nesting Needs: Nest of mud stuck to a vertical surface with overhang as protection, e.g., bridge or cliff.

Eastern Phoebe
Habitat: Woods, farmlands, suburbs.
Food: Insects in air or on ground.
Nesting Needs: Nest of mud and moss, under bridge or eaves of house.

Western Kingbird
Habitat: Open areas with some trees or shrubs.
Food: Insects caught in air, some berries. Needs open perches to fly out from.
Nesting Needs: Nests in trees 8–40 feet high.

Eastern Kingbird
Habitat: Open areas with some trees.
Food: Insects caught in air or picked off ground.
Nesting Needs: Nest of bark strips, plant fibers in tree 10–20 ft. high.

Scissor-tailed Flycatcher
Habitat: Open areas with scattered trees.
Food: Insects caught in air or picked off ground.
Nesting Needs: Nest of soft plant materials placed in tree or on telephone pole crossbar.

Blue Jay
Habitat: Woods and suburbs.
Food: Acorns and other nuts, fruit, insects, bird eggs; sunflower and mixed seed at feeders.
Nesting Needs: Nest of twigs and
bark in trees.

Western Scrub-Jay
Habitat: Varied; brushy country, desert scrub, orchards, canyons.
Food: Insects, acorns, bird eggs, frogs, berries; sunflower at feeders.
Nesting Needs: Nests in shrubs.

Black-billed Magpie
Habitat: Open areas with trees and shrubs, farmlands, gardens, parks.
Food: Insects, berries, bird eggs, carrion, mostly on ground; suet and mixed seed at feeders.
Nesting Needs: Large domed nest of thorny twigs in top of tree or shrub.

American Crow
Habitat: A variety of habitats from country to city.
Food: Wide variety of foods; opportunistic.
Nesting Needs: Bulky nest of sticks placed high in treetop or trunk fork.

Purple Martin (male)
Habitat: Open areas, often near water.
Food: Insects caught in air.
Nesting Needs: East of Rockies, nests only in colony-type birdhouses; in West may nest in single birdhouses, saguaro cactus, or tree hole.

Tree Swallow
Habitat: Open areas near woods and water.
Food: Insects caught in air, berries.
Nesting Needs: Existing tree hole or birdhouse; uses feathers in nest lining.

Cliff Swallow
Habitat: Open areas near cliffs, bridges, out-buildings.
Food: Insects caught in air, sometimes berries.
Nesting Needs: Nest of mud built on cliff, bridge, in culvert. Nests in colonies.

Barn Swallow
Habitat: Open country near barns, bridges, or docks.
Food: Insects caught in air or off water surface.
Nesting Needs: Nest of mud built on side of bridge or inside barn or out-building.

Black-capped Chickadee
Habitat: Woods, farmlands, suburbs.
Food: Insects, seeds, berries; suet and sunflower at feeders.
Nesting Needs: Can excavate cavity in soft, rotted wood of standing tree, or uses existing hole or birdhouse.

Carolina Chickadee
Habitat: Woods, farmlands, suburbs.
Food: Insects, seeds, berries; suet and sunflower at feeders.
Nesting Needs: Can excavate cavity in soft, rotted wood of standing tree, or uses existing hole or birdhouse.

Mountain Chickadee
Habitat: Open coniferous forests in mountains.
Food: Insects, seeds, berries; suet and sunflower at feeders.
Nesting Needs: Can excavate cavity in soft, rotted wood of standing tree, or uses existing hole or birdhouse.

Chestnut-backed Chickadee
Habitat: Coniferous or mixed woods.
Food: Insects and seeds; sunflower and suet at feeders.
Nesting Needs: Can excavate cavity in soft, rotted wood of standing tree, or uses existing hole or birdhouse.

Plain Titmouse
Habitat: Sparse pinyon-juniper and oak woodlands.
Food: Seeds, acorns, insects from trees or on ground; suet and sunflower at feeder.
Nesting Needs: Existing natural cavity in tree or birdhouse.

Tufted Titmouse
Habitat: Woods and suburbs.
Food: Insects, berries, seeds; suet and sunflower at feeders.
Nesting Needs: Existing natural cavity in tree or birdhouse.

Red-breasted Nuthatch
Habitat: Coniferous woods.
Food: Insects, seeds; suet and sunflower at feeders.
Nesting Needs: Can excavate hole in dead tree, or uses existing hole or birdhouse.

White-breasted Nuthatch
Habitat: Deciduous and mixed woods.
Food: Nuts, seeds, acorns, insects; suet and sunflower at feeders.
Nesting Needs: Existing cavity in tree or birdhouse.

Cactus Wren
Habitat: Deserts and semideserts with cactus.
Food: Eats insects, spiders, lizards on ground, also seeds and berries.
Nesting Needs: Large globular nest placed in cactus or other thorny plant.

Carolina Wren
Habitat: Forest understory, vines, woodlands in suburbs.
Food: Insects and tree frogs on or above ground; sunflower at feeders.
Nesting Needs: Nests in natural cavity, birdhouse, or brush pile.

Bewick's Wren
Habitat: Thickets, brush, open woodlands, suburbs.
Food: Insects and spiders on or above ground.
Nesting Needs: Existing natural cavity.

House Wren
Habitat: Woods edges, mountain forests, aspen groves, suburbs.
Food: Insects gathered in bushes and on ground.
Nesting Needs: Existing natural cavity.

Eastern Bluebird (male and female)
Habitat: Farmlands and rural yards, open woodlands.
Food: Insects in short grass areas and berries.
Nesting Needs: Natural cavity in tree or birdhouse.

Western Bluebird (male)
Habitat: Forest edges and open woods.
Food: Insects in open areas and berries.
Nesting Needs: Natural cavity in tree or birdhouse.

Mountain Bluebird (male)
Habitat: Mountain meadows, rangeland, sagebrush, coniferous woods.
Food: Insects while hovering or from perches, berries.
Nesting Needs: Natural cavity in tree or birdhouse.

American Robin (male)
Habitat: Variety of habitats, lawns to mountains.
Food: Earthworms, insects, berries.
Nesting Needs: Nest of grasses and mud placed in tree or on ledge of building.

Varied Thrush
Habitat: Moist coniferous woods.
Food: Earthworms, insects on ground, spiders, snails, seeds, berries.
Nesting Needs: Nest of twigs and moss placed on horizontal limb.

Gray Catbird
Habitat: Shrubs, tangled thickets, woods edges, suburbs.
Food: Insects on ground, spiders, grapes, berries.
Nesting Needs: Nest of twigs, grape bark placed in shrub.

Northern Mockingbird
Habitat: Open areas with shrubs, gardens, parks.
Food: Berries, insects, snails, small snakes, lizards.
Nesting Needs: Nest of twigs, moss, leaves placed in dense shrub.

Bushtit
Habitat: Open woods, chaparral, suburbs, parks, gardens.
Food: Insects gleaned from leaves; seeds and fruits; feeders.
Nesting Needs: Gourd-shaped nest of mosses, rootlets, lichens, spider silk suspended from twigs or branches 4–25 ft. high.

Wrentit
Habitat: Chaparral, tangled brush, or dense shrubs.
Food: Insects, caterpillars, small fruits, and berries.
Nesting Needs: Nest of spiderwebs, bark strips, grasses, lined with fine fibers and hair in bush or tall shrub 1–15 ft. high.

Cedar Waxwing
Habitat: Open rural or suburban areas.
Food: Insects and all types of berries.
Nesting Needs: Nest of grasses and mosses placed in tree 5 ft. high.

Phainopepla (female)
Habitat: Desert washes, oak woods, canyons.
Food: Aerial insects and berries, especially mistletoe.
Nesting Needs: Nest of twigs and grasses placed in fork of tree.

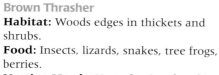

Brown Thrasher
Habitat: Woods edges in thickets and shrubs.
Food: Insects, lizards, snakes, tree frogs, berries.
Nesting Needs: Nest of twigs placed in vine tangle or dense shrubs.

Curve-billed Thrasher
Habitat: Semidesert scrub, suburban yards, parks.
Food: Insects on ground, seeds, berries; fruit at feeders.
Nesting Needs: Nest of twigs and grasses placed in cactus, thorny shrub, small tree.

California Thrasher
Habitat: Coastal chaparral.
Food: Lizards, insects, spiders, berries; fruit at feeders.
Nesting Needs: Nest of twigs and grasses placed in dense bush or small tree.

Yellow Warbler
Habitat: Shrubby areas, especially near water; willows and alders.
Food: Caterpillars of moths, beetles, aphids, and other insects.
Nesting Needs: Nest of milkweed stem fibers and other plant fibers in the fork of a shrub.

Yellow-rumped Warbler
Habitat: Coniferous or mixed forests.
Food: Insects and some berries; suet and fruit at feeders.
Nesting Needs: Nest of twigs and grasses placed 5–50 ft. high.

Common Yellowthroat (male)
Habitat: Dense brushy habitats near wet areas.
Food: Insects, spiders, and seeds gleaned from ground or shrubs.
Nesting Needs: Nest of grasses 1–2 ft. high in shrubs.

Summer Tanager (male)
Habitat: Pine-oak woods, willows and cottonwoods along streams.
Food: Insects, especially bees and wasps; also fruit and berries.
Nesting Needs: Nest of weed stems, bark, grasses 10–35 ft. high in tree.

Scarlet Tanager (male)
Habitat: Large tracts of mature deciduous forests.
Food: Caterpillars and other insects in tree canopy; some wild berries.
Nesting Needs: Nest of twigs, grasses 5–75 ft. high in tree.

Western Tanager (male)
Habitat: Coniferous or mixed forests.
Food: Wasps and other insects in midair; oranges at feeders.
Nesting Needs: Nest of twigs and rootlets 10–65 ft. high in tree.

Northern Cardinal (male)
Habitat: Shrubs near open areas, open woods, suburban yards.
Food: Insects, spiders, seeds, and berries; sunflower at feeders.
Nesting Needs: Nest of twigs and bark strips in dense shrubbery.

Rose-breasted Grosbeak (male)
Habitat: Deciduous woods, mixed shrubs and trees.
Food: Insects, seeds, tree buds, fruit; sunflower at feeders.
Nesting Needs: Nest of twigs placed 5–25 ft. high in tree.

Black-headed Grosbeak (male)
Habitat: Deciduous forests, thickets, pine-oak and pinyon-juniper woodlands.
Food: Tree seeds, berries, insects, spiders; sunflower at feeders.
Nesting Needs: Nest of twigs and rootlets placed 4–25 ft. high in shrub or tree.

Blue Grosbeak (male)
Habitat: Open areas with shrubs, roadsides, hedgerows, farmlands.
Food: Insects, seeds, and fruits on or above ground.
Nesting Needs: Nest of rootlets and grasses placed in shrub or tangle of vines.

Lazuli Bunting (male)
Habitat: Shrubs and low trees in open areas, often near water.
Food: Insects and seeds near ground.
Nesting Needs: Nest of grasses in thicket, shrub, or small tree.

Indigo Bunting (male)
Habitat: Brush or low trees in open areas, overgrown fields.
Food: Insects, seeds, berries on or near ground.
Nesting Needs: Nest of leaves and weed stems in shrub, tangle, or small tree.

Painted Bunting
(male) **Habitat:** Brush, clearcuts, mesquite, rangeland, thickets.
Food: Seeds and insects on or near ground.
Nesting Needs: Nest of grasses and leaves in shrub or small tree.

Eastern Towhee (male)
Habitat: Open woods with shrub understory.
Food: Insects, spiders, lizards, seeds, berries on or near ground; mixed seed at feeders.
Nesting Needs: Nest of leaves and bark strips built in shallow depression in ground.

Spotted Towhee (male)
Habitat: Open woods with shrub understory.
Food: Insects, spiders, lizards, seeds, berries on or near ground; mixed seed at feeders.
Nesting Needs: Nest of leaves and bark strips built in shallow depression in ground.

California Towhee
Habitat: Scrub or suburban yards, parks.
Food: Seeds and insects on or near ground; mixed seed at feeders.
Nesting Needs: Nest of twigs, grasses placed on or near ground.

Chipping Sparrow
Habitat: Grassy areas, open woods, lawns, parks.
Food: Insects and seeds on ground; mixed seed at feeders.
Nesting Needs: Nest of grasses placed in dense shrub or evergreen.

Lark Sparrow
Habitat: Open woods, farmlands, roadsides, suburbs.
Food: Mostly seeds on ground, some insects.
Nesting Needs: Nest of grasses and rootlets placed on ground in tall grasses or other protection.

Song Sparrow
Habitat: Dense shrubs at edges of open areas such as fields, lawns, streams.
Food: Seeds, insects, some berries on or near ground; mixed seed at feeders.
Nesting Needs: Nest of grasses on ground or in shrub or small tree.

White-throated Sparrow
Habitat: Coniferous and mixed woods, brushy areas.
Food: Seeds, insects, fruit on or near ground; mixed seed at feeders.
Nesting Needs: Nest of grasses placed on ground near base of small tree or shrub.

Golden-crowned Sparrow
Habitat: Mountain thickets and shrubs, brushy areas.
Food: Seeds, leaves, flowers, fruit, insects on or near ground; mixed seed at feeders.
Nesting Needs: Large nest of grasses on ground or sloping bank.

White-crowned Sparrow
Habitat: Varied, wet meadows, shrub borders, gardens, parks.
Food: Seeds and insects on or near ground; mixed seed at feeders.
Nesting Needs: Nest of moss and grass placed in depression in ground.

Dark-eyed Junco
Habitat: Woods, bogs, mountains above tree line, brush.
Food: Seeds on ground and off trees; mixed seed at feeders.
Nesting Needs: Nest of moss and grass placed in depression in ground.

Red-winged Blackbird (male)
Habitat: Marshes, meadows with tall grass.
Food: Insects and seeds; mixed seed at feeders.
Nesting Needs: Nest of reeds and grasses attached to taller grasses or shrubs.

Yellow-headed Blackbird (male)
Habitat: Marshes.
Food: Insects and seeds, often in agricultural areas.
Nesting Needs: Nest of reeds and grasses attached to tall reeds and shrubs.

Meadowlarks (Western shown)
Habitat: Meadows, grasslands.
Food: Insects and seeds on ground.
Nesting Needs: Builds a domed nest of grasses on ground in tall-grass areas.

Brewer's Blackbird (male)
Habitat: Wet meadows, shrubby stream edges, roadsides, parks.
Food: Seeds, insects, and fruit on or near ground.
Nesting Needs: Nest of twigs and grass on or just above the ground in a shrub.

Boat-tailed Grackle (male)
Habitat: Parks, lake edges, salt marshes.
Food: Seeds, insects, fruit, crustaceans, fish; mixed seed at feeders.
Nesting Needs: Nest of grasses, reeds, and mud or cow dung placed 3–12 ft. high in shrub or tree.

Great-tailed Grackle (female)
Habitat: Open land with some trees; parks, ranches, urban areas.
Food: Seeds, insects, fruit, crustaceans, fish; mixed seed at feeders.
Nesting Needs: Nest of grasses, reeds, and mud or cow dung placed in shrub or tree.

Common Grackle
Habitat: Open areas with some trees; parks, urban yards, farmlands.
Food: Seeds, insects, fruit, crustaceans, fish; mixed seed at feeders.
Nesting Needs: Nest of grass and mud placed in tree.

Orchard Oriole (male)
Habitat: Orchards, open woods, wetlands, parks, streamside trees.
Food: Insects, fruit, tree blossoms, flower nectar; sugar water at feeders.
Nesting Needs: Shallow pouchlike nest of plant fibers woven to a horizontal fork of a branch.

Baltimore Oriole (male)
Habitat: Deciduous trees near openings, such as parks, gardens, roads.
Food: Insects, fruits, flower nectar; sugar water and oranges at feeders.
Nesting Needs: Suspended nest of plant fibers hung from branch tips.

Bullock's Oriole (male)
Habitat: Deciduous trees near openings, such as parks, gardens, roads.
Food: Insects, fruits, flower nectar; sugar water and oranges at feeders.
Nesting Needs: Suspended nest of plant fibers hung from branch tips.

Purple Finch (male)
Habitat: Mixed woods, coniferous forests, lower mountain slopes, suburbs.
Food: Seeds, tree buds, berries, insects on or above ground; sunflower at feeders.
Nesting Needs: Nest of twigs and grasses placed 5–60 ft. high in tree.

Pine Siskin
Habitat: Coniferous or mixed woods, shrub thickets, suburbs.
Food: Conifer seeds, weed seeds, insects, flower buds, and nectar; sunflower and thistle at feeders.
Nesting Needs: Nest of grasses and twigs placed 3–50 ft. high in tree.

House Finch (female and male)
Habitat: Urban areas, suburbs, parks, canyons, semiarid brush.
Food: Seeds, blossoms, buds, and fruits; sunflower at feeders.
Nesting Needs: Nest of twigs and grasses placed in trees, shrubs, hanging plant baskets.

Lesser Goldfinch (male)
Habitat: Woods edges, roadsides, gardens, parks.
Food: Seeds, flower buds, berries; sunflower and thistle at feeders.
Nesting Needs: Nest of bark strips, moss, plant stems 2–30 ft. high in shrubs or trees.

American Goldfinch (male)
Habitat: Open areas with some shrubs and trees, farms, gardens, suburbs.
Food: Seeds, berries, insects; sunflower and thistle at feeders.
Nesting Needs: Nest of plant fibers and caterpillar webbing 4–20 ft. high in tree.

Evening Grosbeak (male and female)
Habitat: Mixed and coniferous woods, open areas with trees and shrubs, suburbs.
Food: Tree seeds, fruit, nuts, insects, tree sap; sunflower at feeders.
Nesting Needs: Nest of twigs, lichens, roots 20–100 ft. high in tree.

Resources

Societies

Conservancy Purple Martin Society
3090 55th Terrace, S.W.
Naples, FL 34116-8034

National Bird-feeding Society
P.O. Box 23
Northbrook, IL 60065-0023
Phone: 847-272-0135
Fax: 847-498-4092
E-mail: birdseye1@aol.com

The Nature Society
Purple Martin Junction
Griggsville, IL 62340
Phone: 217-833-2323

North American Bluebird Society
P.O. Box 74
Darlington, WI 53530
Phone: 608-329-7056

Purple Martin Conservation Association
Edinboro University of Pennsylvania
Edinboro, PA 16444
Phone: 814-734-4420
Fax: 814-734-5803
E-mail: jhill@vax.edinboro.edu

Purple Martin Society of Illinois
8921 Royal Drive
Burr Ridge, IL 60521-8332
Phone: 630-655-2028
E-mail: hobb99e@Prodigy.com

Books

Basic Birding

Stokes, Donald W. and Lillian Q. 1979. *Stokes Guide to Bird Behavior,* Vol. 1. Boston: Little, Brown.
————. 1983. *Stokes Guide to Bird Behavior.* Vol. 2. Boston: Little, Brown.
————. 1989. *Stokes Guide to Bird Behavior.* Vol. 3. Boston: Little, Brown.
————. 1996. *Stokes Field Guide to Birds: Eastern Region.* Boston: Little, Brown.
————. 1996. *Stokes Field Guide to Birds: Western Region.* Boston: Little, Brown.
————. 1996. *Stokes Beginner's Guide to Birds: Eastern Region.* Boston: Little, Brown.
————. 1996. *Stokes Beginner's Guide to Birds: Western Region.* Boston: Little, Brown.

Basic Gardening

Wyman, Donald. 1971. *Wyman's Gardening Encyclopedia.* New York: Macmillan.

Plant Identification Guides

Craighead, John, Frank Craighead, Jr., and Ray Davis. 1963. *Rocky Mountain Wildflowers.* Boston: Houghton Mifflin Company.
McKenny, Margaret, and Roger Tory Peterson. 1968. *Field Guide to Wildflowers, Eastern and North-Central Region.* Boston: Houghton Mifflin Company.
Niehaus, Theodore, and Charles Ripper. 1976. *Pacific States Wildflowers.* Boston: Houghton Mifflin Company.
Niehaus, Theodore, Charles Ripper, and Virginia Savage. 1984. *Southwestern and Texas Wildflowers.* Boston: Houghton Mifflin Company.
Stokes, Donald W. 1979. *Stokes Guide to Nature in Winter.* Boston: Little, Brown.

Symonds, George W. D. 1950. *The Tree Identification Book.* New York: William Morrow & Company.

———. 1963. *The Shrub Identification Book.* New York: William Morrow & Company.

Birdhouses, Bird Feeders, Birdbaths, Hummingbirds

Fryling, Charles, Jr., Neil Oldenwald, and Thomas Pope. 1993. *Attracting Birds to Southern Gardens.* Dallas: Taylor Publishing Company.

Halpin, Anne. 1996. *For the Birds.* National Wildlife Federation.

Henderson, Carrol L. *Woodworking for Wildlife.* Minnesota Department of Natural Resources Nongame Wildlife Program, St. Paul, MN.

———. 1986. *Landscaping for Wildlife.* Minnesota Department of Natural Resources Nongame Wildlife Program, St. Paul, MN.

Kress, Stephen W. 1985. *The Audubon Society Guide to Attracting Birds.* New York: Charles Scribner's Sons.

Martin, A., Arnold Nelson, and Herbert Zim. 1951. *American Wildlife and Plants.* New York: Dover.

Stokes, Donald W. and Lillian Q. 1987. *Stokes Bird Feeder Book.* Boston: Little, Brown.

———. 1989. *Stokes Hummingbird Book.* Boston: Little, Brown.

———. 1990. *Stokes Complete Birdhouse Book.* Boston: Little, Brown.

———. 1991. *Stokes Bluebird Book.* Boston: Little, Brown.

Stokes, Donald W. and Lillian Q., with Ernest Williams. 1991. *Stokes Butterfly Book.* Boston: Little, Brown.

Stokes, Donald W. and Lillian Q., and Justin L. Brown. 1997. *Stokes Purple Martin Book.* Boston: Little, Brown.

Lawns and Pesticides

Briggs, Shirley A., and Rachel Carson Council. 1992. *Basic Guide to Pesticides.* Bristol, PA: Taylor & Francis.

Schultz, Warren. 1989. *The Chemical-Free Lawn.* Emmaus, PA: Rodale Press.

Magazines

Birder's World, 720 East 8th St., Holland, MI 49423

Bird Watcher's Digest, P.O. Box 110, Marietta, OH 45750

Wild Bird, P.O. Box 6040, Mission Viejo, CA 92690

Black-eyed Susans attract goldfinches and sparrows with their seeds.